Recipes for Gatherings from
Mrs. Sundberg's
KITCHEN

by Holly Harden

Adventure Publications, Inc.
Cambridge, MN

Dedication

For Michael and Deborah, who taught me—among all the other things—about gathering

Acknowledgments

Mrs. Sundberg and I are most grateful to the following:

The good people at Adventure Publications for their hard work, creative input, dedication and care

Tim Trost, the artist whose work has brought the best of life to these pages

Garrison Keillor and our dear friends at A Prairie Home Companion, for giving a nod and lifting it up

The Forest Lake Writers' Workshop, for their steadfastness and rounds of applause

Mr. Sundberg and the kids, for the enthusiasm, support and help cleaning up—especially with the dishes

The Hansens, the Lunds, the Stendahls and Mr. Ableidinger, for all the dishes passed and recipes shared, the willingness to play, the good conversation, and the friendship which is, and ever shall remain, golden

Illustrations by Timothy T. Trost/www.timtrostudio.com

Cover and book design by Jonathan Norberg

10 9 8 7 6 5 4 3 2 1

Copyright 2015 by Holly Harden
Published by Adventure Publications, Inc.
820 Cleveland Street South
Cambridge, MN 55008
1-800-678-7006
www.adventurepublications.net
Printed in U.S.A.
ISBN: 978-1-59193-541-4

Recipes for Gatherings from
Mrs. Sundberg's
KITCHEN

Table of Contents

Foreword by Garrison Keillor

Mrs. Sundberg is what we in Minnesota call a Good Cook. She is not a culinary institute, not a chef looking to make the cover of *Haute Cuisine* magazine and open a four-star eatery in Soho, Madame San Berge´, where Wall Street moguls wait in line for the sausage scaramouche—no, she is a writer and devoted mother of two teenagers and one post-teen and, as part of the mothering bargain, Mrs. S. has striven to put food on the table that makes her offspring happy. Adolescence is rampant with misery, most of it beyond analysis, and if a truly fabulous hamburger or a handmade pizza can help, then that's what needs to be done. No shouting, no pleading, just some frying and seasoning. And in this book, she imagines those rare lovely occasions when adults of various ages gather around a table to be fed and to entertain each other and perhaps are joined by the hungry young.

Mrs. Sundberg comes from Wisconsin and now lives in Minnesota, states famous for their hearty eaters, people who are not put off by wallops of butter or slabs of pork. There is fine cuisine out here, to be sure—restaurants where the waiters are young college graduates who majored in Gender Studies and bring you large white plates with a tiny piece of something atop basmati rice with swirls of liquefied avocado and offer you fresh pepper from a grinder the size of a Louisville Slugger. Of course you can find cafes that serve real food, but it's hard to find home cooking like meat loaf, pot roast, Spanish rice, sloppy joes, real fried chicken, potato salad, gelatin salads, deviled eggs. If you do find it, the quality varies; Michelin tends not to offer guidance to hashhouses and greasy spoons. So more and more people, when they crave real food, eat at home. This is where Mrs. S. comes in. She lays out a good spread for her relatives, her children and their friends, her writing students, her fellow congregants and classmates, and does it with dispatch, no complaining. She doesn't talk a lot about food. She talks about migratory birds, the Gospel, the American novel, and where she traveled years ago that she can't wait to see again.

Back where I come from, the problem with most dinner parties is not the food, it's the conversation. We were brought up to be listeners, to be agreeable, to not talk about ourselves, and so we tend to be passive guests and to tread carefully and avoid exciting the others. Mrs. S. feels that the cook who does the work deserves to hear more than the sound of chewing and the murmur of mild pleasantries. And so she makes the radical suggestion that the host write out prompt cards and place them under the plates—assigning conversation topics as if her guests were a middle school class. This is going to raise hackles. It raises mine. Lift up my plate and find a card that says, "Tell us about your first kiss"? I would rather walk barefoot across gravel. But an impasse requires stern measures, and if someone else goes first and if the cook has to tell us about her first kiss, then I suppose I can think of something. Meanwhile, the food is waiting on the sideboard and we can smell it, Italian sausage and bean casserole, a longtime favorite.

My first kiss was with Corinne Guntzel. We were in sixth grade, it was Christmas vacation, we were sitting on a toboggan behind her house at the top of a high, nearly perpendicular hill that descended to the Mississippi River, and she said, "My lips are cold." And I pressed my lips against hers. She said, "Thank you, that was nice." Kissing a girl was a large moment for a Sanctified Brethren boy and I felt I was on uncharted ground but then we pushed off on the toboggan and it flew down the slope and slid about fifty feet out on the river ice, a thrilling ride. This has colored my view of moral quandaries ever since. I tend to push off and go flying into them. I don't recommend this, but it's been okay for me. That is all. Your turn.

A Note from Mrs. Sundberg

The Midwest, with its rolling fields and storied forests, lakes wherever you go and rivers running through country and city alike, is my home. Here, the weather can make for long days and nights, whether it's -40 with the wind chill or 103 with a heat advisory. People get cabin fever over the winter months, and heat exhaustion in the summer, and though some of us are snowbirds or have cabins in the cool north, for the most part we're around, and we make the best of things. Everyone has his her ways, and my favorite is getting together with friends for the evening.

When I hear the word "gathering," it feels warm to me, and I imagine firelight and people all 'round—talking and laughing and drinking from glasses and mugs and passing plates of fruit and cheese and small hors d'oeuvres made with shrimp and bacon and water chestnuts and figs. The room is warm and the conversation lively; music is playing somewhere, and what time it is doesn't matter much.

The word calls to mind evenings of my childhood, too, when my parents invited friends over for dinner and blender drinks I tasted in the kitchen while they played cards in the dining room or danced to '50s music in the basement. My brothers and I often stayed up late, listening in our pajamas at the top of the stairs to the music of the '60s and '70s, and to the stories of friends who had stories to tell.

There was clean-up to be done the mornings after those parties—confetti and party horns on New Year's Day, fireworks and marshmallow sticks on the patio the weekend of the 4th, bottles and blankets around the fire pit on cold autumn days. I loved helping clean up, hearing my parents talk about the food, their friends, what kind of dinner they might next host.

Another word comes to mind here. I ran across it recently while looking for a recipe for paella (something I intend to give a whirl one day soon). Somewhere in the great rolling hills of the internet, there it was: "sobremesa." A Spanish noun meaning, literally, "over the table." It's a word meaning the time spent after a meal sitting around with people you care about, time savoring not only the food, but the companionship. The sitting and talking and enjoying after a meal.

The sobremesa is what I remember so well from those long-ago dinner parties and now have come to enjoy with Mr. Sundberg and our own gatherings of friends, and it's built right into the heart of this cookbook. Some of the recipes are mine, and some were shared with me; the ideas are all from parties I've attended or hosted. It's not a "how-to" book as much as "what if," and my hope is that, in the same way every artist or scientist experiments and takes risks, you'll find inspiration here to create a meal—and an evening—your friends will long remember.

It's All Greek to Us

At some point in that long stretch of days of sub-zero temps, when the winds are howling and the snow has drifted up against the house, cabin fever creeps in and can overcome a person. There's always hot chocolate, and something to be said for a good book, but a gathering of friends may be just the thing to lift one's spirit, and a good reason to get the fire going. Make it a casual evening, with a buffet of Greek food and some good wine and nothing but conversation. That's how the Greeks did it—they sat around and ate grapes and drank and talked about the Big Ideas.

Greek Salad

Hummus

Tzatziki (Cucumber Dip)

Pastitsio

Greek Baked Beans

Spanakopita

Netta's Baklava

Honey Syrup

~ A FEW GOOD IDEAS FOR THE EVENING ~

DECOR . . . .

Dim the lights, and go with candlelight on the buffet table and around the room. Pick up a few extra pillows and toss 'em on the floor. You might find some laurel branches at a flower shop or a craft store, and strew them about, and dig out that old bust of Socrates or Aristotle from the attic.

TO KEEP THE CONVERSATION GOING . . . . . .

The Greeks asked questions of each other, and had long conversations which often brought about an answer of sorts. Socratic dialogue, it was called. When you send out invites, request that guests come with a question about a Big Idea of your choosing. Truth, perhaps, or Justice or Mercy. Maybe Happiness. Start 'em off with a question of your own and see where it goes.

SOMETHING TO DO . . . .

Have everyone wear a toga, or arrive dressed as one of the Greek gods. Include a list with a short description of each, i.e., Aphrodite, goddess of Love; Hephaestus, god of Fire. Make a game of guessing who is whom. The person who guesses the most correctly wins the laurel.

WHAT TO DRINK . . . .

Retsina, a Greek wine whose flavor comes from pine resin. It goes well with garlic, and most Greek food, and while it might take some getting used to, it's Greek all the way. Or try Ouzo, which tastes like licorice and is made for sipping. Serve it in small, plain glasses during or after dinner. It's colorless and unsweetened and has a solid flavor that tends to grow on you.

MAKE IT YOUR OWN . . . .

Turn the table into a buffet, and invite people to mingle, recline on the couch, or sit on the floor as they eat. Wherever they're comfortable. When it's time to set out the baklava, put on some Greek folk music, keeping it soft, and let people decide whether they'd rather continue talking or dance awhile.

Greek Salad

1 green pepper, deseeded,
  thinly sliced into rings

1 red onion, finely sliced

1 medium cucumber, sliced

2 oz (a handful) ripe kalamata
  olives, pitted

3 medium or 2 large ripe tomatoes,
  cut in thin wedges

6- or 7-oz slice of feta cheese

Olive oil

½ fresh lemon or juice

Fresh oregano or thyme leaves

Salt and pepper

In a large, flat salad dish or plate, combine sliced vegetables with olives and tomato wedges. Lay slice of feta on top and drizzle with olive oil. Squeeze lemon over, and sprinkle with oregano or thyme and salt and pepper. Feta can be cubed or crumbled, if you prefer.

Hummus

1 can chickpeas

½ cup crumbled feta cheese

1 cup fresh baby spinach

2 T lemon juice

¼ tsp cinnamon

1 T water

Rinse and drain chickpeas. Then, put everything in a blender or a food processor and let 'er rip. To thin it out a bit, add 1 T water. Serve with pita bread or crackers.

Tzatziki (Cucumber Dip)

1 (16 oz) container plain yogurt (nonfat works fine)
1 large cucumber, peeled and seeded
Salt, to taste
2-3 cloves garlic, more if desired
1 T wine vinegar or 1 tsp lemon juice
Freshly ground pepper
2 tsp olive oil

Line a sieve with a double thickness of dampened cheese cloth (a coffee filter will work just fine, too). Spoon in yogurt and set the sieve over a bowl. Refrigerate for 2–3 hours or until yogurt is about half its volume, thick and creamy.

Shred cucumber or cut into julienne strips. Place in a colander in the sink or over a bowl, and sprinkle generously with salt. Mix well and let drain for at least half an hour. Rinse and gently pat between paper towels.

Use a garlic press, and squeeze garlic into a bowl. Mash it with a bit of salt, and add the thickened yogurt, cucumber, vinegar or lemon juice, pepper and olive oil. Mix well. Refrigerate up to 2 days so flavors will mingle. Stir again, and serve with pita bread, or chunks of dense fresh bread from the bakery.

If you're a fan, add 1 T dry dill to the mixture; also, it's a nice variation as a garnish.

Pastitsio

1 lb ground beef
½ cup chopped onion
2 cloves garlic, minced
1 (8 oz) can tomato sauce
¼ cup dry red wine
2 T parsley
½ tsp dried oregano, crushed
¼ tsp salt
¼ tsp cinnamon

4 eggs, beaten individually
3 T butter
3 T flour
¼ tsp pepper
1¾ cups milk, divided
½ cup grated Parmesan
1 cup elbow macaroni, cooked
  and drained

In a large skillet, cook meat, onion and garlic until meat is brown. Drain fat, and stir in tomato sauce, wine, parsley, oregano, salt and cinnamon. Bring to bubbling and reduce heat. Simmer about 10 minutes, and stir meat mixture into one of the eggs and set aside.

For the sauce, melt the butter in a medium-sized saucepan. Stir in flour and pepper, and add 1½ cups of the milk. Cook and stir 'til thick and bubbly, and then give it a minute more. Gradually stir sauce into two beaten eggs. Stir in half of the Parmesan cheese. Toss macaroni with the remaining milk, egg and Parmesan.

In an 8x8x2 baking dish, layer half the macaroni mixture, all of the meat, the remaining macaroni and all of the sauce. Sprinkle with a bit of cinnamon, and bake at 350 for 30–35 minutes or until set. Let stand a bit.

This recipe serves about 6 and is easily doubled.

Greek Baked Beans

1 pound dried gigantes beans (or butter, elephant or large lima beans)

3 bay leaves

1 T olive oil

1 onion, diced

1 carrot, diced

2 ribs celery, diced

4 cloves garlic

Chili pepper flakes, to taste

1 (28 oz) can diced plum tomatoes

1 tsp paprika

1 tsp oregano

Salt and pepper, to taste

¼ cup chopped parsley

¼ cup chopped dill

Cover the dried gigantes beans with water, add bay leaves, and soak overnight. Bring the water to a boil and simmer until the beans are tender, about 30 to 40 minutes. Drain beans, reserving ½ cup of the liquid, and set both aside. Heat the oil in a pan, and add the onion, carrot and celery and cook until tender, about 10 to 15 minutes. Add the garlic and chili pepper flakes and cook until fragrant, a minute or so, and add the tomatoes, paprika and oregano and simmer until the sauce thickens, about 20 minutes. Season the tomato sauce with salt and pepper, to taste. Mix the parsley, dill, beans and the reserved ½ cup of bean water into the tomato sauce. Pour the mixture into a casserole dish and bake at 350 until the top is browned and most of the liquid has evaporated, about 50 to 60 minutes.

Makes about 4 servings.

Spanakopita

1 to 1½ package (10 oz each) fresh whole-leaf spinach, stems removed
1 bunch fresh parsley, chopped
2 bunches green onions, chopped
1 lb shredded mozzarella
1 lb shredded cheddar

⅓ cup dried dill weed
Salt, to taste
1 lb package phyllo pastry
1 cup butter, melted, mixed with ¾ cup olive oil

Combine spinach, parsley, onion, cheeses, dill weed, salt. Set aside.

Remove phyllo sheets from package, keeping unused portions covered to avoid drying.

Brush sides and bottom of a 9x13 pan with butter/oil mixture. (A larger rectangular pan will also work.)

Layer pan with 2 phyllo sheets. Brush with butter/oil, lay down 2 more sheets, and brush once again. Continue until phyllo is half used.

Spread spinach mixture evenly over phyllo sheets. Top with phyllo sheets using same method as for the bottom layers, alternating 2 sheets with butter/oil mixture. Do not cover. Bake at 350 for 35 minutes, or until golden brown. Cut into diagonals, or whatever works for you. If you're feeling creative, try experimenting with different fillings.

Netta's Baklava

¾ lb walnuts, finely ground
½ cup sugar
1½ tsp cinnamon
1-lb package phyllo pastry (thawed)

1 cup unsalted butter, melted
1 T ice water
Whole cloves

Combine nuts, sugar and cinnamon. Set aside. Lay phyllo sheets on a flat surface, and cover with a slightly damp towel to keep 'em from drying out. Brush bottom and sides of a 9x13 pan with melted butter. Lay 2 phyllo sheets in the pan, and brush with butter. Repeat until there are 6 sheets in the pan.

Sprinkle ¾ cup of the nut mixture over, and repeat—adding 2 phyllo sheets after each sprinkling—until the nut mixture is gone. Continue to layer phyllo sheets, 2 at a time, brushing with butter, until all the phyllo is used. You may need to melt a bit more butter, depending on how generous you've been. Brush the top sheet with butter, and sprinkle with 1 T ice water. (This will harden the butter.)

With a sharp knife, cut diagonally through baklava from one corner across to the opposite corner of the pan. Make additional parallel cuts at 1-inch intervals. Turn pan and cut diagonally across again from opposite corner, maintaining the 1-inch intervals and making diamond shapes of the baklava. Put a clove on the center of each one. Helpful: keep a cup of ice water nearby, and dip your fingers before you cut the baklava. This will keep your fingers from sticking to it.

Bake at 350 until the top is golden, about 35 minutes. Pour honey syrup (see following recipe) over top, cool thoroughly, and cover with foil. (Start making the syrup about 10 minutes after you slide the baklava into the oven.) Let stand several hours until syrup is absorbed.

Honey Syrup

1 cup water
1 cup sugar
1 tsp lemon juice
1 stick cinnamon
2 whole cloves
1 cup honey
1 T brandy

Bring everything but the honey and brandy to a boil, and cook over medium heat until the thermometer hits 230, about 25 minutes or so. Remove from heat, add honey and brandy, and stir well. Remove the cinnamon stick before you pour the syrup over the pastry.

20

HOW IT ALL WENT

Had our friends over Saturday, and it was a good time. It was cold outside, too cold for togas, but pretty much everyone wore one, and what a sight to behold. The Stendahls wore pale blue-striped togas and sandals, and apologized for not wearing white, but all they had were sheets they'd saved for painting the house. The Hansens wore togas, too, but they'd packed away their summer shoes, so they were both wearing snowmobile boots, which they left at the door. Mr. Lund wore a toga, too, but Mrs. Lund said she felt a cold coming on and didn't want to risk it, and dear Mr. Ableidinger opted out, citing fears of a "wardrobe malfunction."

Everyone admired the table, full up with pita bread and tzatziki, Greek salad and beans. The guests brought wine and a dish to pass, and we had a lovely assortment of olives, cheeses and lots and lots of figs. It didn't take long for mere discussion to morph into a Great Conversation.

The topic for the evening was, "Are You Happy or Content?" and after a good long while, we passed around the baklava, and we all agreed for the most part that contentment is like a river and happiness like the sun. Mr. Ableidinger asked whether the Greeks really throw plates and dance after a good meal. I said yes, and he said, "Opa!" and tossed a paper plate into the air. Then we turned up the music a bit, passed the baklava again, and talked as the candles burned, long into the night.

Lutheran Church Basement Potluck

When it's colder than cold outside, and another Polar Vortex has us counting our blessings, it's time to gather together and enjoy some company and take the focus off the weather outside. If you're lucky, it'll be a day of Old Testament skies—dark and cloud-filled and everything edged in blue. Light some candles in the window, and invite your guests to bring a hotdish or salad or Jell-O to pass, and some good thoughts to share in an evening together at the table.

Tuna Noodle Casserole

Ham Casserole

Adah's Chicken Hotdish

Orange Pineapple Cream Mold

Blueberry Streusel Coffeecake

Rhubarb Crisp

Pecan Pie Bars

~ A FEW GOOD IDEAS FOR THE EVENING ~

DECOR . . . .

Wear an apron. Hang a portrait of Martin Luther on the wall. Gather up some kitschy, iconic décor at a local thrift shop.

TO KEEP THE CONVERSATION GOING . . . .

Ask, in the invitation, that guests to bring along their favorite passage from the Bible, or the Talmud, or the Koran, or any verse they find meaningful or provocative or just downright confusing. Invite each person to share his or her passage over dinner, and have at it.

SOMETHING TO DO . . . .

Request that people "dress Lutheran." Whatever that means to them. They might go all "church lady" or wear a choir robe or their oldest sweater. After dinner, pass out the Bingo cards and play awhile. Prizes can include flour sack towels, in the corners of which you've stitched Lutheranisms like, "Here I stand, I can do no other, so help me God." Or the common table prayer. Or, simply, "Amen." Other prizes? Aprons. A few nice ties. Potholders. Wooden spoons. And mini-Bibles, for the glove compartment.

WHAT TO DRINK . . . .

Send 'round a pitcher of lemonade before and during dinner, or serve it hot if you're inclined, and brew some good strong coffee, too. Set out cream, maybe a few flavors, and sugar, too. And offer up a bit of red wine after dinner, in paper cups.

MAKE IT YOUR OWN . . . .

Each time anyone talks about the weather, that person has to put a clothespin on their shirt collar. Send leftovers home with guests. Use Cool Whip containers, or recyclable plastic containers you've bought or saved from take-out orders. Pass around a basket for donations to a local cause.

Tuna Noodle Casserole

4 T butter, divided
½ cup breadcrumbs
2 cups elbow macaroni or noodles
1 cup sour cream
3 T flour
½ tsp salt
⅛ tsp pepper

1 (10 oz) can condensed cream of mushroom soup
⅛ tsp basil (or tarragon)
¼ cup pimiento, chopped
2 (6 oz) cans light chunk tuna in water, drained

Butter a 3-quart casserole. Melt 1 T butter in a small skillet and stir in breadcrumbs and sauté until golden brown. Cook noodles or macaroni in lightly salted water according to package directions, and drain. Empty sour cream into a large bowl. Fold in macaroni.

Melt 3 T butter in a saucepan. Stir in flour, salt and pepper; cook until bubbly.

Add soup and basil. Cook, stirring until mixture thickens, and add sauce to noodles and sour cream, folding continuously. Mix in pimiento and tuna and pour into a buttered casserole.

Sprinkle with breadcrumbs. Bake at 350, about 20 minutes.

Ham Casserole

2 cups cooked, cubed ham
2 cups diced, cooked potatoes
1 can whole kernel corn, drained
¼ cup fresh minced parsley
1 T chopped onion
¼ cup butter

⅓ cup flour
1¾ cup milk
⅛ tsp pepper
4 oz shredded cheddar cheese
  (or Velveeta)

Combine first four ingredients in a bowl and set aside. Sauté onion and butter for a few minutes in a saucepan. Add flour and stir well. Add milk and pepper and bring to a boil. Cook and stir for 2 minutes. Pour over ham mixture and stir well. Pour into an 11x7x2 baking dish. Cover and cook at 350. After 20 minutes, sprinkle cheese over. Bake another 5 minutes or so uncovered.

Adah's Chicken Hotdish

5 cups cut-up cooked chicken
1 can cream of mushroom soup
1 can cream of chicken soup
1 cup milk
1 cup chicken broth

8 oz shredded cheddar cheese
1 onion, chopped
1 (7 oz) package elbow macaroni, uncooked
1 stick butter, melted

Mix all of the above together in a large baking dish. (You may wish to sauté the onion in a bit of butter beforehand for flavor.) Refrigerate overnight. Let sit out half an hour before baking, covered, at 350 for an hour. Bake a few more minutes uncovered to brown-up the top.

Orange Pineapple Cream Mold

2 (11 oz) cans mandarin oranges, drained, divided
2 envelopes unflavored gelatin
1 cup orange juice with pulp
1 cup boiling water
1 (14 oz) can sweetened condensed milk
1 (16 oz) container sour cream
1 (8 oz) can crushed pineapple, drained
¾ cup chopped walnuts
Lettuce leaves

Line bottom of 6-cup mold with desired amount of orange segments. Set aside.

In a large bowl, sprinkle gelatin over orange juice, let stand 1 minute. Add boiling water and stir until gelatin is dissolved. Add sweetened condensed milk and sour cream, mix well. Fold in pineapple, nuts and remaining orange segments. Turn into prepared mold, and chill 4 hours or so until set. Place onto lettuce and garnish as desired.

Refrigerate leftovers. Makes 10–12 servings.

You can make this one in a pretty bowl and sprinkle extra mandarin orange wedges and walnuts on the top.

Blueberry Streusel Coffeecake

¾ cup sugar
½ cup butter
3 eggs
1 tsp vanilla extract
2 cups flour mixed with
   1½ tsp baking powder
8 oz sour cream, mixed with
   1 tsp baking soda
2 cups blueberries

Topping

1 cup packed brown sugar
2 tsp ground cinnamon
1 cup chopped pecans

Beat sugar and butter together until light and fluffy. Beat in eggs and vanilla. Gradually add flour mixture. Stir in sour cream mixture. Spread half the batter into a greased 9x13 pan. Sprinkle evenly with the blueberries. Blend the topping ingredients together and spread half the mixture evenly over the blueberries. Spoon the remaining batter evenly and then sprinkle with remaining topping. Bake in 350 oven for 40–50 minutes or until wooden toothpick inserted in center comes out clean.

Rhubarb Crisp

4 cups thinly sliced rhubarb
1½ cups sugar
3 T cornstarch
Dash salt
½ tsp cinnamon
2 beaten eggs
¼ cup half-and-half or milk
1 cup quick oats
¼ cup packed brown sugar
¼ cup melted butter

Place rhubarb into a 9-inch baking pan. Sift together sugar, cornstarch, salt and cinnamon. Sprinkle evenly over rhubarb. Combine eggs and half-and-half; pour over rhubarb and stir it all to blend it well. Combine oats, brown sugar and butter. Mix and sprinkle over. Bake at 350 for 30 minutes or until center is set. Serve warm with vanilla ice cream.

Makes 8 servings.

Pecan Pie Bars

1 can crescent rolls
½ cup chopped pecans
½ cup sugar
½ cup corn syrup
2 T butter or margarine, melted
1 tsp vanilla
1 egg, beaten

Unroll dough and press in bottom and ½ inch up the sides of a 9x13-inch pan. Firmly press dough together at the perforations to seal. Bake 8 minutes at 350.

Combine remaining ingredients in a medium bowl. Pour over partially baked crust. Bake 18–22 minutes longer or until golden brown (mine took 20 minutes).

Cool completely, about 1 hour, and cut into bars.

Enjoy!

HOW IT ALL WENT

Had our friends over Saturday, and it was a good time. People began arriving at 6:00, and we all gathered in the kitchen. After a while it got crowded, and that was fine. The Stendahls brought tater tot hotdish, and the Hansens brought pickled herring and beets, and Mr. Ableidinger picked up rolls from the Scandinavian bakery. I served it all family style, and my gosh, it was good. Then Mr. S passed out Bingo cards and agreed to be caller, and I think we had more fun in the next few hours than everyone else in town put together. Somewhere along the way, we got into a fine discussion about the difference between spirituality and religion. Mr. Hansen felt strongly that you need spirituality if you practice a religion, but you don't need religion to have spirituality. We all pretty much agreed.

Mrs. Stendahl got "Bingo" seven or eight times; Mr. Stendahl didn't get one. By the time we were ready for dessert, I'd passed out all the prizes—chocolate bars, work gloves, flour sack towels and a few jars of jam. Mrs. Lund brought peach pie, and I cut it up, along with the coffeecake, and we ate enough pie and drank enough coffee to keep us going 'til midnight, but there was church in the morning and a cold drive home. Our goodbye took a good half hour, as goodbyes tend to do if you live in Minnesota. I hugged each of my friends, and Mr. S and I stood on the porch and waved as our friends drove away, containers of leftovers and all.

Garlic and Love

It was Augustus Saint-Gaudens who said, "What garlic is to food, insanity is to art." Couldn't have said it better myself. You need a little seasoning now and then to make things interesting. Being in love is like that. There's something to be said for routine, and being able to count on someone, but there's always room for a bouquet of roses, a poem written in longhand and read aloud while standing on the back deck as the sun sets, or a good love story. Yep. A little spice goes a long way.

Roasted Garlic

Pasta Carbonara

One-Pot Bean and Pasta Stew
(Pasta e Fagioli)

Homemade Meatballs

Red Pepper Sauce for Pasta

Rustic Italian Bread

Italian Sausage and
Bean Casserole

Big Heart Cake

~ A FEW GOOD IDEAS FOR THE EVENING ~

DECOR . . . .

Roses. Buy a couple dozen red or purplish or salmon-colored sweetheart roses, and trim them down, arrange them in small vases with baby's breath and ribbons and place them throughout the house. Set out plates here and there piled with all sorts of chocolates. And don't forget the mints.

TO KEEP THE CONVERSATION GOING . . . . . .

Invite everyone to come prepared to tell the story of their first kiss, and to tell a love story, real or not. But real is better. Make a game of guessing which stories are truth and which are fiction, and the winner takes home a bouquet of roses. Or a box of chocolates, tied with a ribbon.

SOMETHING TO DO . . . .

Place a quote or poem about love under each plate. During the meal, invite guests, one at a time, to read their piece aloud for discussion. I would include a poem or two, maybe something from the Brownings, or a Shakespearean sonnet. Talk about love in the context of the quote or poem, and see what comes up.

WHAT TO DRINK . . . .

Wine, wine and more wine. Invite your guests to bring a bottle of their favorite. Everyone might be asked to choose a bottle of wine to share featuring a picture on the label of the place they'd most like to go. Words to describe an activity might also suffice. After dinner, and with dessert, open a bottle of limoncello, a delicious liqueur served cold.

MAKE IT YOUR OWN . . . .

Play tango music, quietly, in the background, or perhaps some opera. A tenor, or several. After dinner, switch to violin. Or cello.

Roasted Garlic

Start with a dozen heads of garlic.

Peel and discard the papery outer layers of the whole garlic bulb, leaving intact the skins of the individual cloves of garlic. Using a sharp knife, slice horizontally about ⅓ inch from the top of cloves, exposing the individual cloves of garlic.

Place the garlic heads in a muffin pan, cut side up. Drizzle a couple teaspoons of olive oil over each exposed head, rubbing the olive oil over all the cut, exposed garlic cloves. Cover the bulbs with aluminum foil. Bake at 400 for 30–35 minutes, or until the cloves feel soft.

Allow the garlic to cool a bit. Use a small knife cut the skin slightly around each clove. Use a cocktail fork or your fingers to pull or squeeze the roasted garlic cloves out of their skins, or let your guests do it. Serve in a bowl as is, or mash it up a bit and spread over warm French bread.

If not serving as an appetizer, mix it in with Parmesan and pasta.

Pasta Carbonara

3 large eggs (as many as 2 to 4 work fine)
⅔ cup freshly grated Parmesan cheese
½ to 1 lb bacon
8 oz baby bella mushrooms, sliced
⅓ cup olive oil
2 large cloves garlic, chopped finely
2-4 fresh red chilis (I often use dried)
1 lb dried spaghetti
Black pepper, to taste

Combine the eggs and Parmesan in a small bowl and whisk until smooth. Set aside. Fry the bacon in a small frying pan until crisp. Remove and break into 1-inch pieces. Gently brown the mushrooms in the bacon drippings. Remove. Wipe out pan with paper towel. Combine the oil, garlic and chilis in the pan and cook over low heat, making sure the garlic doesn't burn. It should be a pale straw color. Add bacon and mushrooms and heat on low. Stir occasionally.

Cook the spaghetti in plenty of salted boiling water until al dente. Drain, reserving a small measuring cup of the cooking water. Turn the pasta into a bowl (a warm bowl works well). Remove the chilis from the frying pan and pour remaining contents over pasta, then right away the egg and cheese mixture, along with some of the reserved pasta cooking water. Toss well. The hot pasta cooks the egg. Serve immediately, topping with ground black pepper.

One-Pot Bean and Pasta Stew (Pasta e Fagioli)

1 pound dried cannellini beans
5 slices bacon, diced
2 large yellow onions, sliced thin
3 tsp salt, divided
3 celery stalks, diced

4 garlic cloves, minced
1 bay leaf
5 thyme sprigs
½ pound pasta (cellentani or ditalini)
10 oz baby spinach

Pour the beans into a large mixing bowl and cover with cool water. Let sit at least 6 hours or overnight.

In a heavy stockpot or Dutch oven, fry the bacon over medium heat. Once fat has rendered, remove bacon and set aside. Pour off all put 1 T of fat. Cook onions slowly with ½ tsp of salt until they caramelize and turn golden brown, about half an hour. Add the celery and cook just until the celery is softened, about 3 minutes. Add the garlic and cook until fragrant, about 30 seconds.

Remove half of the onion mixture and reserve with bacon. Pour a cup of water into the pot, scraping up any brown residue. Drain beans and pour them into the pot with the water and onions. Add bay leaf and enough water to cover the beans and onions by an inch. Cover the pot and bake in oven at 325 for an hour. After an hour, check the beans every 15 minutes until they are completely soft.

Return the pot to the stove top on medium-high heat. Add bacon, reserved onions, whole thyme sprigs, remaining salt and dry pasta. Cook, stirring occasionally, until pasta is al dente. Add more water if necessary. Add spinach to the pot and stir until it is wilted. Remove bay leaf and thyme stems. Taste and add more salt and pepper if desired.

Serves 8–10.

Homemade Meatballs

1 lb ground beef

4 slices bread, crust removed, pulled into small pieces

2 eggs

½ cup grated Parmesan or Romano cheese

1 T parsley

1 tsp oregano

1-2 cloves garlic, peeled and chopped fine

½ tsp salt

Dash or two pepper

Dash cayenne pepper

2-3 T olive oil

Place ground beef in a bowl and, using a potato masher, break the meat apart. Add remaining ingredients except oil, and mix and mash well. Using your hands, form meatballs the size of large walnuts or golf balls. Heat meatballs in an oiled skillet, first at medium high, then reduce heat to low, and cook for a good while, turning meatballs every 10 minutes or so until they're nice and brown.

Pour your favorite sauce over and simmer for 45 minutes or so, or until ready to serve.

These meatballs make great sandwiches or appetizers, too.

Red Pepper Sauce for Pasta

1 cup heavy cream
1 cup roasted red pepper puree (you'll need 3 red bell peppers; see below)
½ to 2 tsp dried red pepper flakes
½ tsp salt

Simmer all ingredients for 5 minutes. Pour over pasta or cooked chicken or meatballs.

For red pepper puree: Roast red bell peppers in a 450-degree oven until burned and blistered, about 40 minutes. Wrap in a clean kitchen towel and let steam until cool. Peel off blistered skin; don't worry if some is left on. Remove the stem, seeds and white pith, then puree in blender.

Rustic Italian Bread

3 cups cold water
7 cups bread flour
2 packages quick-rise yeast
1 T salt

Mix ingredients together and let rest 15 minutes. Cut into 7 pieces. Cover. Let sit 10 minutes. Punch down and shape into 7 loaves.

Place on a large, greased baking sheet. Cover. Let rest 20 minutes.

Cut X-marks over dough. Bake at 400 for 45–50 minutes.

Italian Sausage and Bean Casserole

12 slices white sandwich bread

Salt

Ground pepper

2 lbs smoked Polish or
Italian sausage, halved lengthwise,
cut into 2½-inch pieces

2 large onions, chopped

8 cloves garlic, chopped

½ cup tomato paste

1 can (14½ oz) chicken broth

1 cup dry red wine

1 tsp thyme

4 cans (14½ oz) great northern or
cannellini beans, rinsed and drained

Parmesan cheese (to top)

In a food processor, pulse bread until large crumbs form (about 6 cups).
(You can also pull the bread into pieces yourself.) Season with salt and pepper.
Set aside.

Cook sausage, onion, and garlic in a 6-quart heavy-bottom saucepan, stirring
occasionally, until onions are clear and sausage is starting to brown, 15 to 20
minutes. Add tomato paste, broth, wine, thyme and 2 cups water; bring to a
boil. Reduce to a simmer; add beans. Simmer, stirring occasionally, until slightly
thickened but still soupy, about 10 minutes. Stir in 2 cups of the breadcrumbs.
Divide sausage mixture between two 3-quart shallow baking dishes or eight
10-oz ramekins. Top with remaining breadcrumbs. Bake, on a baking sheet, until
topping is golden, about 30 minutes at 375.

Garnish with fresh Parmesan cheese.

Big meals don't require big desserts. After a fine meal of pasta and meatballs and bread, consider serving spumoni, or small bowls of a raspberry gelato. If you prefer something a bit more special, serve slices of this lovely heart cake with a scoop on the side.

Big Heart Cake

1 box cherry chip or strawberry or white cake mix
1 container frosting, pink or white or chocolate
  (or your favorite homemade frosting)
Assorted decorations—nonpareils, candy hearts,
  gumdrops, chocolate kisses

Mix cake according to directions. Pour half of the batter into an 8x8 greased and floured square pan and the other half into an 8-inch greased and floured round pan. Bake according to instructions.

When done and cool, remove square cake and place on large, foil-covered piece of cardboard. Cut round exactly in half and place each half along adjacent sides of the square so it forms a big heart. Frost with frosting and decorate as you wish. Write something fun or naughty on the cake, or cover it with lit candles, and present to your guests.

Enjoy!

HOW IT ALL WENT

Had our friends over Saturday, and it was a good time. We lit up a good number of candles and sat around the table drinking wine and talking. The Stendahls brought assorted cheeses, and the Hansens brought a salad, the Lunds brought olives, and Mr. Ableidinger brought us each a bottle of wine matched to our personalities. Mine was a bottle of riesling from Cupcake Vineyards, and Mr. Sundberg's bottle read "Sycamore Lane," a deep-red wine. Mrs. Stendahl's was simply called "Relax."

The food was wonderful, and we opened several bottles of wine at once and took turns telling love stories long into the night. My favorite was Mr. Hansen's story about how, way back when, he visited the coffee shop in his hometown, and there was this young woman sitting by the window, reading. Her hair was kind of a golden red, and she turned to look at him as he walked in, and she was the most beautiful girl he'd ever seen. He went over to her table. "Is this seat taken?" he asked. "It is now," she replied. She was reading *A Sand County Almanac*, and in town to visit her aunt and uncle on their farm. "That was nearly four decades ago," he said. "Only woman I've ever loved, or ever will." And he put his arm around Mrs. Hansen, and kissed her cheek. He raised his glass. "To love," he said. "True love." We all touched our glasses, and drank, and we stayed there at the table a good long while, eating chocolates and laughing as the candles burned low.

At the Irish Table

You don't have to be Irish to engage in blarney, or swap a tale or two, or make a good cup of Irish coffee. When March rolls around and there are hints of spring in the air, it's time for the wearin' o' the green and a plate piled high with corned beef and collops, and if things go right, you may find yourself doing a jig before the evening is over. The luck o' the Irish be with you.

Blue Cheese Stuffed Mushrooms

Maple Oatmeal Scones

Irish Onion Soup

Corned Beef Sauerkraut Sandwiches

Potato Collops

Colcannon

Irish Whiskey Cake

~ A FEW GOOD IDEAS FOR THE EVENING ~

DECOR . . . .

Use a green tablecloth, and real shamrocks if you can find 'em. Or make your own, and hang a rainbow on the wall leading to a pot filled with gold-wrapped toffee or chocolates.

TO KEEP THE CONVERSATION GOING . . . .

Ask everyone to do some research and come prepared to share a legend, Irish or not. Warriors and leprechauns, faeries and St. Patrick and banshees are all fair game. Or have a go-round, each person sharing what they might do with the pot o' gold at the end of the rainbow.

SOMETHING TO DO . . . .

Play an Irish version of "Who Am I?" by taping the names of famous Irish people to each person's forehead. The idea is to ask questions of each other in order to guess who you are. Or prepare and play a game of Irish-themed trivia. Or, later in the evening after a few Irish coffees, play some Irish music and have a little jig contest. The winners could receive small bottles of whiskey.

WHAT TO DRINK . . . .

Make some Irish coffee. While a fresh pot of coffee is brewing, whip some heavy cream, and add a bit of sugar for sweetness. Chill. Pour 6 ounces of hot coffee into a mug (you might go all out and buy some glass Irish coffee mugs), leaving a bit of room at the top. Stir in a teaspoon of brown sugar and an ounce-and-a-half of your favorite Irish whiskey (Jameson is my favorite), and drop a dollop of whipped cream on top. Enjoy!

MAKE IT YOUR OWN . . . .

Serve up some Irish beer. Dye it green if you're really feelin' it. And while you're at it, make some Irish soda bread and dye that green, too, and serve it with a plate of Irish cheese. Along with dessert, set out a plate of shamrock-shaped sugar cookies frosted green, with gold sprinkles.

Blue Cheese Stuffed Mushrooms

6 large white mushrooms, stems removed

4 oz Cashel Blue Cheese, or something similar

Flour, for dredging

1 egg, beaten

2 T water

Breadcrumbs, for dredging

Oil, for frying

Mixed greens

Vinaigrette dressing

Mustard Meade Dip

½ cup mayonnaise

¼ cup Lakeshore Wholegrain Mustard with Bunratty Meade

½ to 1 tsp chopped fresh dill

Wash mushrooms and dry with paper towel. With a small knife or spoon, stuff mushroom caps with cheese, and dredge in flour. In a small bowl, combine the egg and water to make an egg wash. Dip mushrooms in egg, then in breadcrumbs.

In an electric skillet or deep fryer, heat the oil for deep frying (to about 350). Drop the mushrooms, one at a time, into the hot oil. Cook, turning as necessary with a wooden spoon, until golden brown. Remove each as soon as brown and drain on paper towels.

To serve, place 3 hot mushrooms in the center of a bed of mixed greens that has been drizzled with vinaigrette.

For the dip, combine ½ cup mayo, ¼ cup Lakeshore Wholegrain Mustard with Bunratty Meade, and ½ to 1 tsp chopped fresh dill.

Maple Oatmeal Scones

2 cups flour
1½ cups oatmeal
3 T sugar
1½ tsp baking powder
½ tsp baking soda
½ tsp salt
½ tsp cinnamon
⅛ tsp ginger
1 stick butter
½ cup buttermilk
½ cup maple syrup

½ tsp maple extract
½ tsp vanilla
1 egg
⅓ cup raisins
3 T sugar
⅓ cup chopped pecans, optional

Combine first eight ingredients in bowl and mix thoroughly. Cut in butter until walnut-sized chunks remain. Add buttermilk, maple syrup, maple extract, vanilla and egg, and stir briefly until dough comes together. Add raisins (and pecans if desired) and mix a bit more. Turn dough out onto a lightly floured board and pat evenly into a circle about ¾ inch thick. Cut into pie-shaped pieces. Bake on greased cookie sheet at 375 until light golden brown, about 15 to 20 minutes. To serve, dot with butter, and sprinkle with cinnamon sugar.

If you have no buttermilk, you can substitute yogurt or sour cream one to one, or ½ cup milk plus ½ tsp lemon juice or vinegar.

Irish Onion Soup

2 T unsalted butter

3 large yellow onions, peeled and sliced

2 large red onions, peeled and sliced

4 shallots, minced

3 garlic cloves, minced

2 bay leaves

1 tsp dried basil

1 sprig fresh thyme

1 T dark brown sugar

3 cups beef stock or canned beef broth

1 cup Guinness, or other stout beer

Salt and freshly ground pepper to taste

1 cup (4 oz) shredded Kerrygold Swiss or Blarney Castle cheese, for topping

In a large saucepan over medium heat, melt the butter. Add the onion, shallots, and garlic and cook for 12 to 15 minutes, or until the onions are soft but not browned. Add the bay leaves, basil, thyme, brown sugar, stock or broth, and stout. Bring to a boil, then reduce heat to low and simmer, covered, for 25 to 30 minutes, or until the onions are tender. Season with a bit of salt and pepper.

Preheat the broiler. Arrange 8 1-cup flameproof crocks on a baking sheet, and ladle the soup into the crocks and sprinkle with the cheese.

Place under the broiler, 4 inches from the heat source, and broil for 1 to 2 minutes, or until the cheese melts and starts to brown. Remove from the oven and place a crock in the center of each of 8 serving plates, and serve immediately.

The best reuben I've had was made for me by a boy I had an eye for way back. We'd dated a few times and didn't know much about each other except how drawn we each were, and when he invited me to his home for dinner one Wednesday night before the Lenten church service, I about cartwheeled. It was near St. Patrick's Day, and he was even more Irish than I, so the meal was his specialty. He cooked; I watched. He carefully fried the sauerkraut, then set it aside. Then he fried the corned beef—not crisp, but so it was a little brown and sweet around the edges. Then he assembled the sandwiches in the pan with the hot ingredients, some light rye without caraway seeds, and big slices of Swiss cheese. The bread came out toasted just right, and he poured, without discretion, the most wonderful Thousand Island dressing in a bowl for us to share. He even lit a candle, and we sat there, laughing, dipping our huge sandwiches in dressing while his parents watched the evening news. To this day, I've yet to enjoy a reuben as satisfying.

Corned Beef Sauerkraut Sandwiches

2 (14 oz) cans sauerkraut
2 (12 oz) cans corned beef
¼ lb Swiss cheese
3 T Thousand Island dressing
3 T horseradish mustard

Drain sauerkraut. Chop up the corned beef with a fork. Grate the Swiss cheese. Mix all ingredients together and place in a slow cooker for 2 hours. Serve on party rye.

Potato Collops (a "collop" is a "little bit of food")

3 medium potatoes
1 large onion, chopped
Salt and pepper, to taste
2 T chopped parsley
¼ lb raw bacon, diced
2 T butter
1 cup milk
3 T grated cheese

Pare potatoes and cut into thin slices. Place a layer of potatoes and onion in a greased baking dish. Sprinkle with seasonings, parsley and diced bacon. Dot with butter. Repeat layers until all ingredients are used, finishing with potatoes. Pour in milk and sprinkle top with grated cheese. Cover and bake at 350 for 45 minutes. Uncover and bake until potatoes are done and top layer is brown.

Colcannon

3 cups cooked and mashed potatoes
2 cups chopped, boiled cabbage
Salt and pepper, to taste
4-6 slices bacon (or Irish bacon if you can get it)
1 large onion, chopped
2 cloves garlic, crushed and minced
1 leek, chopped (white and pale green parts only)
4 T butter, divided
1 cup breadcrumbs, scant

Combine potatoes and cabbage together in large bowl. Season to taste with salt and pepper. Sauté bacon in large skillet until crisp. Remove bacon to drain on clean paper towels; sauté onion, garlic and leek in same skillet. Add half of the butter to the skillet and stir in potato and cabbage mixture. Crumble/chop bacon and add half of it to the mixture. Mix and heat through. Transfer to a buttered casserole. Sprinkle with breadcrumbs and dot with remaining butter. Place in 425 oven and bake until lightly browned, about 15 minutes. Sprinkle top with remaining bacon.

Serves 4.

Irish Whiskey Cake

1 (18½ oz) package spice cake mix
1 large (5.1 oz) package instant
  vanilla pudding mix
¾ cup milk
4 large eggs
½ cup oil
¾ cup Irish whiskey
⅓ cup chopped walnuts

Glaze

1 stick butter
1 cup sugar
1 tsp water
2 tsp whiskey

Blend cake mix and pudding mix in large bowl. In a separate bowl, blend milk, eggs, oil and whiskey, then add to dry ingredients. Mix for 2 minutes by hand, and make sure to scrape the sides of the bowl. Pour into a lightly greased tube pan. Sprinkle with walnuts. Bake approximately 1½ hours at 300 until lightly browned on top. Remove from oven and let cool in pan.

For the glaze: melt butter in a saucepan, and add sugar, water and whiskey; stir. Boil gently for 10 minutes, then remove from heat and cool for 3 minutes. Pour over cake while it is still in the pan. Let cool for 1 hour, then remove cake from tube pan right side up, and place on cake plate. Best results if left to sit overnight.

Enjoy!

HOW IT ALL WENT

Invited our friends over Saturday, and it was a good time. We served up reubens and some good blue cheese, a bit of soup and some whiskey cake, and there were no complaints. Nice to try something new now and then, and Mrs. Lund brought two loaves of soda bread, first time she ever made it, and was it ever fine.

I was the only one in the group who has been to Ireland, and I didn't have a slideshow to present, or even a photo album, but I passed around a few pictures, and told the story of the pirate queen Grace O'Malley, and described the pubs and the good stews and breads served up all over, and how kind the people are everywhere you go. I told them about the Cliffs of Moher, how they took my breath away with the sheer drop to the sea, and the green of the grass and the sky and salt smell and the birds.

I put on some Irish folk music and served some Irish coffee, and we got to telling stories of our travels 'round the world. Stories of the Caribbean, Africa, China and Italy. Mr. Stendahl's story of his two-week visit to Russia was my favorite, and we all agreed that the Hansens' visit to Alaska counts as world travel. We never did get to playing the game I'd planned, or to the Irish jig contest at which Mr. Sundberg rolled his eyes, but that's fine by me. Some nights are for dancin', and some are for stories. Good to have options, for sure.

Rhubarb

As spring rolls into summer, people are out cleaning up their lawns, planting gardens, and talking with each other amid the flowers and greenery. It's been a long winter, and it's time to open all the windows and have a little fun. Variety is said to be the spice of life, but it seems right and fine, now and then, to celebrate just one thing, and let's make it rhubarb, everything rhubarb, for a late springtime dinner with friends.

Rhubarb Bread

Arugula Salad with Strawberry
Rhubarb Vinaigrette

Rhubarbecued Ribs

Rhubarb Pork Chop Casserole

Rhubarb Wild Rice Pilaf

Rhubarb Cake

Raspberry Rhubarb Pie Bars

Scandinavian Rhubarb Pudding

Rhubarb Sauce

~ A FEW GOOD IDEAS FOR THE EVENING ~

DECOR . . . .

Arrange wildflowers and rhubarb in milk bottles and place them around the house. Look for rhubarb-scented soap, or candles, too.

TO KEEP THE CONVERSATION GOING . . . .

It's springtime, and there's a lot to talk about. Gardens, summer plans, cabin stories. Avoid talking about winter. It's over. A meal of everything with rhubarb in it will spark a conversation of its own.

SOMETHING TO DO . . . .

Time for open windows and a cool breeze. Sit out on the deck or patio, or eat at the picnic table. In the invite, include a request for limericks about rhubarb. And make a rule that—apart from the limerick—no one can say the word "rhubarb" all evening. Here's an example: There once was a man with a garden/that was neat, and as green as Eden/his rhubarb was quite fine/with it he made strong wine/and drank too much and dozed off while weedin'.

WHAT TO DRINK . . . .

Rhubarb wine. If you look, you'll find some, but you gotta look. Or whip up a batch of rhubarb slush: In a big pot, cook 8 cups of chopped rhubarb with 8 cups of water, 3 cups of sugar and ½ cup lemon juice. Simmer 10–15 minutes or so, and strain. Discard the solids, and add 1 small package strawberry Jell-O (not instant) and 2 cups of vodka, and stir 'til dissolved. Freeze in a 5-quart ice cream pail. Scoop into glasses and serve with 7-Up or Sprite.

MAKE IT YOUR OWN . . . .

Order screen-printed T-shirts with rhubarb stalks on the front, one per person. Or send each person home with a jar of rhubarb sauce you made yourself. Or some rhubarb pie. Or a bundle of rhubarb itself.

Rhubarb Bread

1½ cups brown sugar

⅔ cup oil

1 tsp vanilla

1 egg, slightly beaten

1 tsp salt

1 tsp soda

2½ cup flour

Pinch cinnamon

1 cup sour milk (add 1 tsp vinegar
    or lemon juice to 1 cup milk; mix
    well and let stand for 5 minutes)

1½ cup diced raw rhubarb

½ cup chopped walnuts

1 tsp vanilla

Topping

⅓ cup granulated sugar mixed
    with 1 T melted butter.

Mix brown sugar, oil, vanilla and egg together. Sift salt, soda, flour and cinnamon together. Add dry ingredients alternately with milk to other mixture. Fold in rhubarb and nuts. Fill 2 lightly greased loaf pans ⅔ full. Sprinkle with topping. Bake at 325 for 1 hour.

Arugula Salad with Strawberry Rhubarb Vinaigrette

1 cup chopped fresh rhubarb
1¼ cups chopped fresh strawberries
3 large shallots, coarsely chopped
1 T sugar
⅓ cup red wine vinegar
¾ cup canola oil
¼ tsp Dijon mustard
1 bunch arugula
12 whole strawberries, cut in half
4 oz goat cheese or feta

Simmer first five ingredients in small saucepan until tender, about 10 minutes. Puree, strain into large bowl, and cool.

Whisk in canola oil and mustard.

Fill bowl with arugula leaves, chopped. Sprinkle with berries and cheese, and pour dressing over.

Rhubarbecued Ribs

4 lb lean, meaty beef short ribs
½ cup water
½ tsp seasoned salt
1 cup sliced rhubarb
1 (1½ oz) envelope onion soup mix
⅓ cup honey

⅓ cup chili sauce
¾ cup rose wine
⅓ cup water
½ tsp basil
⅛ tsp pepper

Place ribs in 9x13 pan. Add ½ cup water and sprinkle with seasoned salt. Cover with foil and bake at 350 for 2 hours. Combine remaining ingredients in a sauce pan and simmer about half an hour. Pour over ribs and bake another half an hour, uncovered. Baste several times and place on serving platter. Garnish with greens. Serves 6.

Rhubarb Pork Chop Casserole

4 pork chops
1 T cooking oil
Salt and pepper, to taste
2½ to 3 cups breadcrumbs

3 cups rhubarb, cut up
½ cup brown sugar
¼ cup flour
1 T cinnamon

Brown pork chops in oil; add salt and pepper. Remove to platter. Mix ¼ cup pan drippings with breadcrumbs. Reserve ½ cup crumbs and sprinkle remaining crumbs into 9x13-inch baking dish. Combine rhubarb, sugar, flour and cinnamon. Spoon half over the breadcrumbs. Arrange pork chops on top. Spoon remaining rhubarb mixture over chops. Cover with foil and bake at 350 degrees for 45 minutes. Remove foil, sprinkle remaining crumbs. Bake 15 minutes longer.

Rhubarb Wild Rice Pilaf

¼ cup slivered almonds
2 T olive oil
1 cup chopped sweet onion
2 cloves garlic, minced
2 cups chopped rhubarb
½ cup white wine
½ cup golden raisins

1 tsp ground cinnamon
¼ tsp cayenne pepper
2 T honey
1 T soy sauce
1 cup cooked wild rice
1 cup cooked long-grain white rice

Spread almonds onto a baking sheet and toast at 400 until fragrant, 7–10 minutes.

Heat oil in a large skillet over medium-high. Sauté onion in hot oil until just translucent, 5 to 7 minutes. Add garlic and sauté until fragrant, about a minute. Mix rhubarb into onion and garlic and sauté until softened a bit, about 2 minutes more. Stir wine, raisins, cinnamon and cayenne pepper into rhubarb mixture; cover the skillet with a lid, reduce heat to medium-low and simmer until rhubarb is tender to the bite but still firm, 5 to 8 minutes. Add honey and soy sauce; stir. Mix wild rice and white rice into the rhubarb mixture; cook and stir until rice is heated through. Top with toasted almonds.

Serves about 6.

Raspberry Rhubarb Pie Bars

3¼ cups flour
1 tsp salt
1 cup butter
¾ cup plus 1-2 T milk
1 egg yolk
2 cups sugar
⅓ cup cornstarch
5 cups fresh raspberries, or frozen unsweetened raspberries, thawed and drained
3 cups sliced fresh rhubarb, or frozen rhubarb, thawed and drained

Icing

1¼ cups powdered sugar
½ tsp vanilla extract
5 to 6 tsp milk

In a large bowl, combine flour and salt; cut in butter until crumbly. Whisk ¾ cup milk and egg yolk; add to flour mixture, tossing with a fork until dough forms a ball. Add more milk, 1 T at a time, if necessary. Divide dough into two portions, one slightly larger than the other; wrap each in plastic wrap. Refrigerate for an hour or so until easy to handle.

Roll out larger portion of dough between two large sheets of lightly floured waxed paper into an 18x13 rectangle. Transfer to an ungreased 15x10x1 baking pan. Press onto the bottom and up the sides of pan; trim pastry to edges of pan. In a large bowl, combine sugar and cornstarch. Add raspberries and rhubarb; toss to coat. Gently pour into pastry.

Roll out remaining dough; place over filling. Fold bottom pastry over edge of top pastry; seal with fork. Prick top with fork. Bake at 375 for 45–55 minutes. Cool.

For icing, combine powdered sugar, vanilla and enough milk to achieve a drizzling consistency; drizzle over pie. Cut pie into squares. Makes 2 dozen bars.

Rhubarb Cake

½ cup shortening

½ cup brown sugar

1 egg

1 cup sour milk (add 1 tsp vinegar or lemon juice to 1 cup milk; mix well and let stand for 5 minutes)

1 tsp vanilla

2 cups flour

1 tsp soda

½ tsp salt

1½ cups chopped rhubarb

½ cup sugar

½ cup chopped walnuts

1 tsp cinnamon

In medium bowl, cream together shortening and brown sugar. Stir in egg, sour milk and vanilla. Add flour, soda and salt. Combine well and fold in rhubarb.

Pour into a greased 9x13 cake pan. Mix together ½ cup sugar, walnuts and cinnamon and sprinkle over batter. Bake at 350 for 50 minutes.

Scandinavian Rhubarb Pudding

1½ pounds rhubarb
1½ cups water
½ cup sugar
½ tsp vanilla

3 T cornstarch
1 cup heavy cream
¼ cup sugar
1 tsp vanilla

Trim rhubarb and cut into ½-inch slices. Combine with water and sugar and simmer until soft. Stir in vanilla. Blend cornstarch with a bit of cold water to make a smooth, stiff paste, and stir into rhubarb. Cook for 5 minutes, stirring constantly, until thickened and clear. Pour rhubarb into glass serving dish and chill. When you're ready to serve the pudding, whip the cream until frothy; add sugar and vanilla and whip until stiff. Spread over pudding and serve.

Rhubarb Sauce

2 cups fresh rhubarb, cut into 1-inch pieces
1 cup water
½ cup sugar

Simmer rhubarb, water and sugar in a small saucepan for 15 minutes or until rhubarb softens and sauce thickens. Makes 2 cups. For thicker sauce, use a bit less water. Serve on ice cream, pancakes, just about anything.

Enjoy!

HOW IT ALL WENT

Invited our friends over Saturday, and it was a good time. I got a few calls after I sent out the invites. Mrs. Stendahl wanted a recipe for rhubarb and wild rice, and Mr. Stendahl thought it was a joke. Nope. When the good Lord gives you lemons, you make lemonade; when what you get is rhubarb, well . . . you have at it. And we did.

We sat outside on lawn chairs and the weather was lovely. A good hour of sun and warm, and a breeze, and we ate ribs Mr. Sundberg did up on the grill, and enjoyed some of Mr. Ableidinger's rhubarb pudding, which we ate before the ribs were done, and that felt right to me.

The sky grew dark in the distance as we ate, and the clouds were spectacular. We sat together and drank rhubarb slush and Mr. Stendahl sang a song he wrote about rhubarb, and it was to the tune of "My Bonnie Lies Over the Ocean." Part of it went, "Oh blow the winds o'er the ocean/And blow the winds o'er the sea/Oh blow the winds o'er the ocean/And bring back my rhubarb to me . . ." It was supposed to be funny, and it was. We all joined in on the refrain, and it became quite sweet, and lovely, and there was thunder, but we just sat there and sang awhile, before the raindrops fell and we made a mad dash, plates and all, for the house.

At Play on a Hot Summer Evening

It gets as hot here in the summer as it does cold in the winter, and no one wants to do much but head to the lake or nap in the hammock. Just like in the dead of winter, it helps to have something to look forward to, and who could say no to a picnic dinner under the stars?

Sour Cream Fruit Dip

The Freshest Salad Ever

Overnight Lettuce Salad

Crock Pot Barbecue Chicken

Soda Pop Biscuits

Five Cup Fruit Salad

Mrs. Sundberg's Mother's
Strawberry Angel Food Dessert

Snickerdoodles

~ A FEW GOOD IDEAS FOR THE EVENING ~

DECOR . . . .

String lights over the patio, and put out some bright-pink potted geraniums. Fill small, colorful balloons with water and freeze 'em. Place the balloons in a large tub and add soft drinks, bottled water or other beverages. The balloons take the place of ordinary ice and can be used again and again.

TO KEEP THE CONVERSATION GOING . . . .

Talk about summers when you were young. Where did you live and who were your neighbors?

SOMETHING TO DO . . . .

Plan a grown-up treasure hunt. Plant clues, and make it a bit of a challenge. If your friends have kids, invite them along. Plan a meal of hot dogs and chips for the kids, and send them off to plan a skit to perform later in the evening.

WHAT TO DRINK . . . .

Lemonade. With fresh lemons. Wine coolers. Wine. Water. Invite guests to bring a mixed drink to share, something tropical and fruity. Or get a keg of root beer and have some vanilla ice cream on hand, just in case.

MAKE IT YOUR OWN . . . .

Dine al fresco. This means outside, on the patio or deck. Make sure there are lots of bubbles. Invite people to go barefoot, if so inclined. Get out the guitar, or invite guests to bring one.

Serve ice cream cones, or banana splits.

Sour Cream Fruit Dip

1 small (3.4 oz) package vanilla instant pudding
1 cup milk
1 cup sour cream
1 tsp vanilla

Combine ingredients well. Let sit awhile in the fridge, and serve with your favorite fruit. Strawberries and bananas work just fine.

The Freshest Salad Ever

1 bulb fennel
1 sweet Vidalia onion
2 oranges

Cut up just the white part of the fennel as you would celery, in half moons, and place in a medium-sized bowl. Slice up a Vidalia onion (use half as much onion as fennel, about ⅓ cup). Mix with the fennel.

Peel two oranges, removing as much of the soft white pith as you can. With a small knife, section off slices over bowl, letting the juices drip in.

Add salt and pepper if you wish, though it's not necessary.

Mix and serve.

Overnight Lettuce Salad

3 cups shredded lettuce
6 hard-boiled eggs, sliced and lightly salted and peppered
2 cups thawed frozen peas (or fresh, if you've got 'em)
3 cups shredded lettuce
8 oz shredded cheddar cheese (or more)
½ to 1 lb bacon, fried and crumbled
2 cups mayonnaise or salad dressing to cover (I use 1 cup each)
A sprinkle each of sugar, salt and pepper
1 bunch green onions, sliced
Paprika

Spread 3 cups lettuce over bottom of 9x13 glass baking dish. Scatter sliced egg over the lettuce, and then add the peas, and cover with another 3 cups shredded lettuce. Sprinkle cheese over, and the bacon goes on top of the cheese. Gently spread mayo over the bacon. Sprinkle lightly with sugar, salt and pepper. Garnish with sliced green onions and paprika.

Refrigerate overnight, up to 24 hours, a minimum of 6.

Crock Pot Barbecue Chicken

1 bottle (18 oz or so) barbecue sauce (Sweet Baby Ray's is a fine choice)
¼ cup vinegar
1 tsp red pepper flakes
¼ cup brown sugar
1 tsp garlic powder
4-6 chicken breasts

Combine everything but chicken. Place chicken in crock pot (frozen is fine).
Pour sauce mixture over chicken and cook on low for 4 to 6 hours.

Soda Pop Biscuits

4 cups Bisquick
1 cup sour cream
1 cup 7-Up
½ cup butter, melted
Dash salt

Mix Bisquick, sour cream and 7-Up. Dough will be very soft. Knead and fold
until coated with baking mix. Pat dough out and cut biscuits using a round
dough cutter or a cookie cutter.

Melt butter in bottom of 9x13 pan or casserole or cookie sheet. Place biscuits on
top of melted butter and bake at 435 for 12 to 15 minutes or until golden brown.

Five Cup Fruit Salad

    1 cup sour cream
    1 cup mandarin oranges, drained
    1 cup crushed pineapple, drained
    1 cup coconut
    1 cup mini-marshmallows

Mix. Chill. Serve.

Mrs. Sundberg's Mother's Strawberry Angel Food Dessert

    2 (3 oz) packages strawberry Jell-O
    2 (10 oz) packages sliced frozen strawberries
    2 T sugar
    2 pinches salt
    1 pint whipping cream, whipped
    1 angel food cake, torn in pieces

Dissolve Jell-O in 2½ cups boiling water. Stir in thawed berries, sugar and salt. Cool until Jell-O begins to thicken. Fold in whipped cream. Cover bottom of 9x13 pan (a glass one works best) with half of torn cake. Spoon over half of berries and cream mixture. Make another layer using the rest of the cake and top with remaining berries and cream. Refrigerate 4–5 hours to set. Add dollop of whipped cream or fresh strawberries when serving.

Snickerdoodles

1 cup shortening (butter works fine, too)
2 cups sugar, divided
2 eggs
2¾ cups flour
2 tsp cream of tartar
1 tsp baking soda
¼ tsp salt
1 T cinnamon

Mix shortening, 1½ cups sugar and eggs thoroughly. Add flour, cream of tartar, soda and salt; mix well. Shape dough in 1-inch balls. Roll in a mixture of ½ cup sugar and 1 T cinnamon. Place 2 inches apart on greased baking sheet. (Or place on a foil-lined sheet, which you don't have to grease—just slide off and replace with another sheet.) Bake 8–10 minutes at 400. The cookies will puff up a bit then flatten.

Makes about 6 dozen.

HOW IT ALL WENT

Had our friends over Saturday, and it was a good time. Was a hot one, up in the 90s, and humid. We gathered late in the day and had barbecued chicken and biscuits and fruit while we sat watching the sun sink into waves of summer heat. Mr. Sundberg lit the lanterns, and that soft light lit our faces and I brought out dessert—angel food with strawberries, and cream, and a little Jell-O in there to hold it all together. "One of my mother's recipes, and a favorite when I was young," I said, as I served it up.

Long-ago summers became the topic for the night, and Mr. Lund went on awhile about how he and his brother would climb anything that rose up toward the sky. Mrs. Stendahl talked about swimming in the river near her house, and Mr. Sundberg told how he and his father built the *premiere* tree house, complete with a door and four windows and a shingled roof. There was mostly silence from Mr. Ableidinger, until we'd all quieted a bit. "Though I was an only child, I never felt much alone. Spent my time outdoors, out there in the quiet." Away in the distance, an owl hooted, and somewhere farther off, a dog barked. I poured more coffee all 'round and Mr. Hansen picked up his guitar, and began to play something that sounded like a lullaby. At that moment, in the afterglow of sunset, among good friends and empty dessert plates, I felt pure contentment, and it felt real fine.

Mexican Fiesta

Now I've never been to Mexico, but I like the idea of it, and I hope to visit there one day. In the meantime, a Mexican dinner with a group of friends is as close as I can get, and summer is a good time to make it happen. Send out packets of chili peppers with a little note attached, announcing the date and time, and invite people to dress casual, and to bring along some salsa and chips.

Tortilla Soup

Taco Dip

Mexican Lasagna

Homemade Refried Beans

Taco Bake

Corn Muffins

Baked Flan

~ A FEW GOOD IDEAS FOR THE EVENING ~

DECOR . . . .

Decorate with small piñatas and cacti (buy enough to send one home with each guest/couple). You can create handmade flowers for the table with tissue and pipe cleaners and top the table with a red, white and green tablecloth. Consider chili peppers as your motif, and use 'em everywhere.

TO KEEP THE CONVERSATION GOING . . . .

In the invite, announce a salsa contest. Have everyone bring some salsa and after the appetizers are served, cast a vote and the winner gets first swing at the piñata.

SOMETHING TO DO . . . .

Before the party, buy a piñata and fill it with whatever you like. Candy is always a sure bet, but make it a surprise and throw in a few fishing lures, spools of yarn, little wrapped Mexican fruitcakes. (Lutefisk is a thought, but, nah.) Maybe a few unplayed scratch-off tickets, or lip balm. Hang the filled piñata outside where there's room for fun, and have guests go at it with a broomstick as limbo music or mariachi tunes play in the background.

WHAT TO DRINK . . . .

Margaritas, margaritas, margaritas. Offer three kinds—regular, strawberry and peach or coconut or something blue. Basic margaritas require 8 oz tequila, 4 oz triple sec and 8 oz fresh lime juice. Combine and shake well. Dip glasses in salt, and fill 'em with ice. Strain the drink into the glasses and there you go.

MAKE IT YOUR OWN . . . .

You could hire a mariachi band to show up and play for an hour, but a CD will work just fine. Mexican polka music sounds a lot like German polka music, and you might suggest a bit of dancing. Or, after all that food, you might prefer a more quiet game of Mexican Train dominoes. You'll have to educate yourself before hand, but it's fun to learn a new game with a group of friends. Especially when there are refills on the margaritas.

Tortilla Soup

16 oz sour cream
1 pint (16 oz) jar salsa
1 (15 oz) jar queso dip
1 (15 oz) can black beans (drained)
1 (16 oz) can chili beans (hot)
2 (15 oz) cans corn (drained)
1 (26 oz) family size can chicken and rice soup
1 soup can of water
4 chicken breasts cooked and diced

Combine all of the above in a large soup pot. Bring to a gentle boil, then reduce to a simmer. If you wish to serve this recipe as a dip, leave out the can of water.

Taco Dip

16 oz French onion dip
1 (16 oz) jar picante sauce
1 T taco sauce
1 small onion, chopped
1 green pepper, chopped
1 head lettuce, shredded
8 oz sharp cheddar cheese, grated
1 small tomato, diced
1 bag nacho cheese Doritos

Combine first three ingredients and spread on a serving plate. Layer onion, green pepper, lettuce, cheese, tomato and a handful or two of crushed Doritos. Serve with Doritos or tortilla chips.

Mexican Lasagna

1½ lbs ground beef
1 can refried beans
1 package taco seasoning
1 package lasagna noodles
2½ cups water
2½ cups chunky salsa
1 (8 oz) carton sour cream
1 (8 oz) package shredded cheddar cheese
1 cup shredded mozzarella
Black olives, as many as you wish
Chopped onion, as much as you wish

Mix raw beef, beans and taco seasoning. Grease 9x13 cake pan or casserole and alternate ⅓ meat mixture at a time with uncooked noodles, using 3 layers of noodles. Add water and salsa on top. Bake covered at 350 for 1½ hours. Remove from oven. Spread sour cream over, and sprinkle with cheeses, and olives and onions if you choose. Bake uncovered 10–15 minutes until it looks about right.

Homemade Refried Beans

1 (15 oz) can pinto beans
1 or 2 T olive oil
1 large sweet onion
2-3 cloves garlic
Salt and pepper
Flour tortillas
Salsa, cheddar cheese, avocado, tomatoes, optional

Drain pinto beans not quite dry.

Heat a cast iron skillet over medium heat and then add 1 or 2 T of olive oil. Chop up onion and garlic, the more the merrier, if you ask me. Sauté onion and garlic until translucent then add the beans. Keep heat at about medium and when warmed up, mash them right in the pan. Keep heating, stirring to prevent scorching, until the mixture reaches a smooth, but not too runny, consistency. Add salt and a lot of pepper. Warm a flour tortilla over a warm burner, place a nice amount of the refried beans in the center along with your favorite salsa and some grated cheese. Chopped avocado or tomatoes are good additions. Roll and serve with some Mexican rice or a taco salad.

Taco Bake

1 lb ground beef, browned and drained
1 envelope taco seasoning
1 can corn, drained
1 (15 oz) can tomato sauce
3 cups shredded cheddar cheese
2 cups baking mix (I lean toward Bisquick)
1 cup milk
2 eggs
Cornmeal

Mix the ground beef with the taco seasoning, corn and tomato sauce. Spread into a 9x13 pan. Sprinkle cheese evenly over.

Stir baking mix, milk and eggs together until well blended. Pour/spread over cheese layer. Dust with cornmeal.

Bake at 350 uncovered for about 35 minutes. (Poke a hole in the middle to make sure it's done.)

Serve with beans, salsa, sour cream and tortilla chips.

Corn Muffins

½ cup flour
½ cup cornmeal
3 T sugar
½ tsp baking soda
½ tsp salt
1 egg
8 oz sour cream

Combine flour, cornmeal, sugar, soda and salt. Set aside. Stir together egg and sour cream, and mix in with flour mixture until just moistened. Fill muffin cups ⅔ full and bake at 400 for 15 to 18 minutes.

Baked Flan

⅔ cup sugar
1 (14 oz) can sweetened condensed milk
2 cups heavy cream
1 cup milk
5 eggs
2-3 tsp vanilla

In a small nonstick saucepan, heat the sugar over medium heat. Swirl pan occasionally to distribute sugar until it is dissolved and begins to brown. Stir only a bit. Lift the pan over the burner a few inches and continue to brown the sugar until it becomes a dark golden brown. Pour caramelized sugar into a 1½-quart casserole dish or a large loaf pan, and swirl to coat the bottom of the pan evenly.

Blend together sweetened condensed milk, cream, milk, eggs and vanilla. Blend on high for one minute. Pour over the caramelized sugar.

Place the filled casserole dish into a larger pan filled with an inch or so of hot water.

Bake at 350 for 50 to 60 minutes, or until set.

Enjoy!

HOW IT ALL WENT

Invited our friends over Saturday, and it was a good time. The sun is still high in the evening, but things have cooled down a bit, and with everyone at their cabins, it'd been a while since we've had people over. It was nice to have an evening together, and a memorable one at that, thanks to Mrs. Stendahl's salsa, and Mr. Ableidinger's hat.

The salsa contest was more fun than I'd imagined. Everyone entered, and it was all homemade except for Mr. Ableidinger's, which he picked up at a Whole Foods store nearby. There was mango salsa, and garlic salsa, and pineapple salsa. Some was mild, and some was zesty, and it was all good. Mrs. Stendahl's was so hot that we had to refill Mr. Stendahl's margarita. Twice. That's when we put on the music and went outside to hit the piñata.

Everyone took a turn swinging a bat while blindfolded, but it was Mr. Stendahl who leveled the rainbow-colored donkey and sent miniature candy bars and raffle tickets flying. There was a great cheer, and everyone scrambled to gather up the goods. By the time the Mexican lasagna was ready, we were hungry, and we enjoyed dinner for a long while. We took our dessert to the living room, and there Mr. Ableidinger told us all about his cruise to Mexico a few years back, and how he drank drinks from coconuts, and felt like he was in Paradise. He dozed off shortly after, there in the recliner, with a smile on his face and his sombrero slightly off-kilter.

Hawaiian Pontoon Picnic

Spending some time on the lake followed by dinner on the beach is a fine way to say farewell to summer. And when you have a crowd, what better place is there for dinner than a ride on the ol' pontoon? This gathering combines the best of summer into an evening—a boat ride on a lake, some good food with friends, a campfire with songs, a sunset over the lake. Aloha, I say.

Hawaiian Cheesy Bread

Caribbean Jerk Salmon

Pork Adobo

Caribbean Rice

Spicy Crab Cakes

Papaya Chutney

Hawaiian Pineapple Dessert

~ A FEW GOOD IDEAS FOR THE EVENING ~

DECOR . . . .

Whether you're on the beach or in the backyard, tiki torches will create a lovely mood for a summer evening outdoors. Gather wood for a campfire, too, and consider assembling one of those science-kit exploding volcanoes as a centerpiece on the food table.

TO KEEP THE CONVERSATION GOING . . . .

Specify in the invitation that each person is responsible for learning one Hawaiian word or phrase and sharing it with the group before the evening is over. Example: "Mahalo" (amahalo) is an expression of gratitude in Hawaii, a way of saying "thank you." Like "aloha," it's a word with great spiritual meaning, and suggests the presence of the divine.

SOMETHING TO DO . . . .

Gather together an hour or two before dinner, and take a pontoon ride. If you don't live by a lake, meet at the home of someone in the group who does, or head out to a boat landing and launch from there. Bring pineapple drinks and an appetizer or two, and a ukulele, and sing a few songs as you tour the lake.

WHAT TO DRINK . . . .

Make some sangria. Pour a liter of rose wine into a large pitcher. Add a cup each of rum and of pineapple juice, and ¾ cup lemon juice. Half a cup of sugar is optional. Stir it well. Slice one lemon and one lime into rounds, and peel and cut up a mango, and add to the pitcher. Chill it well, and serve it in hollowed-out pineapples with the tops removed. Paper umbrellas make a nice touch.

MAKE IT YOUR OWN . . . .

Invite everyone to wear Hawaiian shirts, and pick up some leis at a dollar store, or go all out and order some from a local florist. Hawaii has the largest consumption of SPAM per capita, so include it somehow, maybe making it a door prize for the best hula dance.

Hawaiian Cheesy Bread

1 loaf Hawaiian sweet bread
8 oz block of Swiss cheese
3-4 slices red onion, chopped

½ cup butter, melted
3-4 garlic cloves, minced
1 tsp salt

Cut bread diagonally into 1-inch slices to within 1 inch of bottom of loaf. Repeat cuts in opposite direction. Cut Swiss cheese into ¼-inch slices. Cut slices into small pieces and sprinkle into bread. Combine the remaining ingredients and spoon over the bread. Wrap loaf in foil and bake at 350 for 25 to 30 minutes until cheese is melted.

Caribbean Jerk Salmon

1 cup Fiber One cereal
2 T Caribbean jerk seasoning
1 tsp sea salt
1 tsp black pepper
1 lb fresh salmon cut into 4 equal fillets

Line a baking pan with aluminum foil and spray with cooking spray, or use a little butter.

Crush the cereal to the consistency of breadcrumbs, and in a shallow dish mix it with the jerk seasoning, salt and pepper. Dip salmon in mixture, covering completely, and place in baking pan.

Bake at 350, uncovered, for 18 to 20 minutes.

Pork Adobo

Recipe from the Philippines, but it has become a classic Hawaiian dish.

3 lb boneless pork butt, cut into 1-inch cubes
½ cup cider vinegar
¼ cup soy sauce
1 tsp whole black peppercorns
1 T minced garlic
1 T minced fresh ginger
1 bay leaf, crushed
1 T chili pepper flakes

Combine all ingredients in a container. Cover and refrigerate 3 hours or so. Transfer the pork and marinade to a Dutch oven and bring to a boil. Cover and simmer over low heat for 30 minutes. Uncover and simmer another 15 minutes, until the pork is lightly browned. Serve with rice.

Caribbean Rice

2 tsp oil
¾ cup shredded coconut
½ cup minced sweet Vidalia onion
2 cups rice
4 cups chicken broth
1 ripe, firm mango, peeled and cubed
¼ cup fresh chives, minced

Heat oil in a large saucepan and add the coconut. Cook, stirring all the while, until lightly browned. Add minced onion, and cook and stir another minute. Add rice. Stir to coat, and add broth. Bring to a boil. Cover, reduce heat to low, and simmer 25–30 minutes or until rice is tender. Remove from heat, and stir in mango. Garnish with chives.

Spicy Crab Cakes

1 lb fresh crab meat
1 egg
¼ cup mayo
2 T chopped fresh cilantro
1 T Thai chili sauce
½ T cumin

½ cup breadcrumbs (fine)
Pepper, to taste
1 cup cornmeal
2 T butter

Combine everything but the cornmeal and butter. Form into 12 cakes. Coat lightly with cornmeal, and sauté in butter until golden brown.

Serve with papaya chutney.

Papaya Chutney

2 cups papaya, seeded and diced
¼ cup diced onion
½ cup diced red pepper
½ cup sugar

1 tsp allspice
1-2 tsp cider vinegar
½ cup water

Combine all ingredients in a saucepan, and cook until thickened.

Hawaiian Pineapple Dessert

1 yellow cake mix (regular size)
3 packages (3.4 oz each) instant vanilla pudding mix
4 cups cold milk
1½ tsp coconut extract
1 (8 oz) package cream cheese, softened
1 (20 oz) can crushed pineapple, well drained
2 cups heavy whipping cream, whipped and sweetened
2+ cups flaked coconut, toasted

Mix cake batter according to package directions. Pour into two greased 13x9 baking pans. Bake at 350 for 15 minutes or until the cakes test done. Cool.

In a large bowl, combine pudding mixes, milk and coconut extract; beat for 2 minutes. Add the cream cheese and beat well. Stir in pineapple. Spread over the cooled cakes. Top with whipped cream; sprinkle with coconut. Chill for at least 2 hours.

This recipe makes 24 servings and can be frozen.

Enjoy!

HOW IT ALL WENT

Invited our friends over Saturday, and it was a good time. We all agreed to meet over at the Hansens' house on the lake for a ride in their big ol' pontoon boat.

The Hansens are a good-time couple. They travel a lot together, and just built a huge porch onto their house, and spend a lot of time out on the lake. They're about as in love as two people can be, and tend to keep the rest of us laughing. The Stendahls aren't what you'd call a perfect match: he's gentle and shy, while she tends to be a bit ostentatious, and they bicker now and then, which is pretty normal the way I see it. The Lunds are both introverts, and she's a good five years older than he is. He adores her, and she blushes a lot, and they're both into music and art and deep conversation. Mr. Ableidinger is a bit of a mystery. He's a retired teacher, been single as long as we've known him, plays organ at weddings and owns an apple orchard over by the river.

The Hansens served up sangria and we snacked on Hawaiian bread and crab cakes, and we returned to shore happy and hungry and headed over to our place. Mr. Sundberg lit the torches, and the Hawaiian buffet was by the fire pit. We roasted chunks of SPAM in the flames and Mr. Lund played his ukulele, and Mrs. Stendahl did a little hula dance. Everyone said, "Mahalo!" as they left, and they meant it, and we felt it, and it felt just right.

Fall Fondue Party

In his poem "The Wild Swans at Coole," Yeats wrote:

> The trees are in their autumn beauty,
>
> The woodland paths are dry,
>
> Under the October twilight the water
>
> Mirrors a still sky . . .

And that pretty much sums up an autumn evening in these parts. Time to get out the comfort food, and have some friends over for an evening of creative food and good time fun.

Alpine Fondue

Beer Cheese Fondue

Meat Fondue

Chicken and Shrimp Fondue

A Few Good Dipping Sauces

Maple Fondue with Walnuts

Sweet Chocolate Fondue

~ A FEW GOOD IDEAS FOR THE EVENING ~

DECOR . . . .

Decorations don't have to be complicated. Keep it simple. Bring in some beautiful fallen leaves and arrange them under candles, on counters, even use them as coasters. Since a fondue party can be a bit messy, pick up a clear plastic tablecloth, lay it down over your white one, and place leaves in between.

TO KEEP THE CONVERSATION GOING . . . .

Play a game where everyone comes up with three statements about themselves. One of the statements is a lie and two are true. The other players have to guess which statement is fake. Example: I live in Minnesota but was born in Florida. I have a dog that loves women and not men. My side business is decorating cakes.

SOMETHING TO DO . . . .

Fondue is pretty much what you do at a fondue party. The word comes from the French word, "fondre," which means "to melt," and though the Oxford Dictionary says it is a noun, I prefer to use it as a verb, as in "It's your turn to fondue." Fondue is more an event than a dish and involves dipping food into hot sauces or cooking it in broth or oil. Place your fondue pots on the table (most pots come with candles you burn under them to keep them warm). Have guests gather 'round the table and pass around plates of meat and vegetables and fruit, explaining which food goes in which pot.

WHAT TO DRINK . . . .

Have some apple cider on hand, along with a variety of wine and beer. Maybe a seasonal brew from a local brewery. Keep a pitcher of ice water in the fridge. Fondue can be on the salty side.

MAKE IT YOUR OWN . . . .

Invite guests to bring something chocolate for dessert. Or rent a "chocolate fountain"; they are really a sight to see.

Alpine Fondue

12 oz shredded Swiss Cheese
2 T flour
2 garlic cloves, cut in half
1½ cups dry white wine
2 T Kirsch brandy, optional

Toss cheese with flour. Rub inside of saucepan with garlic. Add wine, and heat until bubbles rise to the surface. (Do not boil.) Add ½ cup cheese mixture; stir until melted. Repeat until all cheese has been added. Stir in Kirsch if desired.

Serve hot in a pot with bread chunks. Add a small amount of wine to thin if necessary.

Beer Cheese Fondue

1-lb loaf French bread, cubed
¼ cup chopped sweet Vidalia onion
1 T butter
1-2 tsp minced garlic
1 cup beer
4 cups (16 oz) shredded cheddar cheese
1 T flour
2-5 T half-and-half

Place bread cubes in a single layer in an ungreased 15x10 baking pan. Bake at 450 for 5 to 7 minutes or until lightly crisp, stirring twice.

In a small saucepan, sauté onion in butter until tender. Add garlic; cook a minute longer. Stir in beer, bring to a boil, reduce heat to medium-low. Toss cheese and flour together, and stir into saucepan until melted. Stir in 2 T half-and-half.

Transfer to a small fondue pot or 1½-quart slow cooker. Keep warm, and add additional half-and-half as fondue thickens. Serve with toasted bread cubes.

Makes about 3 cups.

Meat Fondue

1 quart peanut oil
1 (3 lb) beef tenderloin or boneless beef top, cut into 1½-inch cubes
2 (8 oz) packages fresh baby bella mushrooms, gently washed.

When it's time to eat, heat peanut oil in fondue pot over medium heat until oil reaches 350.

Place on warmer to maintain heat. Place beef cubes and mushrooms on serving platters and pass beef and mushrooms around the table. Place 1 or 2 pieces beef and a mushroom or two on fondue fork. Place in hot oil; cook until beef is of desired doneness and mushrooms are tender. Serve with dips and sauces.

Chicken and Shrimp Fondue

2-3 lb boneless, skinless chicken breasts
8-16 oz raw shrimp
8 cups chicken broth
½ cup sliced green onion
1 tsp grated fresh ginger
Dash or two of pepper

Partially freeze chicken. Slice chicken crosswise into thin, bite-sized strips. Set aside. Peel and devein shrimp. Set aside.

Combine broth, onion, ginger and pepper in a large saucepan. Bring mixture to a boil. When ready to serve, fill fondue pot with mixture and return to boiling.

Use a fondue fork to dip chicken or shrimp into broth; cook to desired doneness. Serve with dipping sauces.

A Few Good Dipping Sauces

Aioli

½ cup mayonnaise
1-2 garlic cloves, minced
3 T olive oil
¼ tsp salt

In small bowl, combine mayonnaise and garlic. Whisk in the olive oil and salt until well blended.

Curry

¾ cup mayonnaise
1 tsp lemon juice
2 tsp curry powder
⅛ tsp ground ginger

Combine ingredients in small bowl.

Steak

½ cup ketchup
2 T Worcestershire sauce
½ tsp garlic salt

Combine all ingredients in a small bowl.

Horseradish

⅓ cup mayonnaise
⅓ cup sour cream
1 T prepared horseradish
1 T Dijon mustard

Combine all ingredients in small bowl.

Southwestern

¾ cup bottled chili sauce
2 T finely chopped onion
1 T prepared horseradish
¼ tsp garlic salt
3 T snipped fresh cilantro
4 tsp lime juice
1 jalapeño chili pepper, seeded and chopped fine
4 dashes bottled hot pepper sauce

In a small bowl, combine all ingredients.

A Few Good Dipping Sauces

Sesame-Ginger

1 cup soy sauce
2 T Dijon mustard
2 T honey
2 T water
½ tsp toasted sesame seeds
½ tsp grated fresh ginger

Combine, cover and refrigerate.

Just Plain Good

1 cup sour cream
1 package dry onion soup mix
3 egg yolks
1 tsp lemon juice
½ tsp Worcestershire sauce
White pepper, to taste
Salt, to taste

Blend sour cream and soup mix; add egg yolks, lemon juice, Worcestershire sauce and seasonings. Cook over low flame, stirring constantly until sauce starts to thicken slightly. Do not boil. Remove from heat and continue stirring as sauce thickens. Allow to cool before serving.

Note for all dips: Cover each dip or sauce tightly. Refrigerate until serving time.

Maple Fondue with Walnuts

4½ tsp cornstarch
1 cup evaporated milk
¾ cup maple syrup
½ cup plus 1 T corn syrup
6 T finely chopped walnuts

3 T butter
¾ tsp vanilla extract
Cubed pound cake
 and assorted fresh fruit

In a medium saucepan, combine cornstarch and milk until smooth. Stir in maple syrup and corn syrup. Bring to a boil over medium heat; cook and stir for 2 minutes or until thickened. Remove from the heat. Stir in walnuts, butter and vanilla. Transfer to a small fondue pot and keep warm. Serve with cake cubes and fruit. Makes about 1½ cups.

Sweet Chocolate Fondue

⅔ cup light corn syrup
½ cup heavy whipping cream
8 oz German sweet chocolate, chopped

In a microwave-safe bowl, combine corn syrup and cream. Cover and microwave on high for 2 to 2½ minutes or until mixture just comes to a boil, stirring twice. Stir in chocolate until melted. Transfer to a fondue pot and keep warm. Serve with cookies and/or fruit.

Makes about 2 cups.

Enjoy!

HOW IT ALL WENT

Invited our friends over Saturday, and it was a good time. The best thing about a fondue party is that it's a bit unconventional. We started with bread and cheese fondue, and then I changed the fondue pots and brought out plates of beef, chicken and shrimp, and a platter of vegetables the Hansens brought.

We played the truth or lie game while we ate, and laughed hard as we played. It was hard to believe that Mr. Ableidinger was a gymnast in high school, and that the Lunds are taking tango lessons, and that Mrs. Stendahl wears footie pajamas. When Mr. Sundberg stated that he had a tattoo of a walleye on his butt, I had to contain myself. Funny thing is, they all believed it and thought he hadn't really played tuba in high school.

We spent the rest of the evening in the family room, where Mr. Sundberg built up the fire and we all discussed our artistic endeavors. Mrs. Stendahl had revised a poem she'd written a while back, about a girl who loved someone from afar and no one ever knew, and it was soulful and I cried a little, and Mr. Lund played "Stairway to Heaven" on his guitar. Mrs. Lund showed us the rug she is hooking, and Mr. Sundberg played "Home Sweet Home" on his harmonica. And me? I plugged in the chocolate fountain and brought in a plate of shortbread and strawberries. I'm not much of a musician, preferring to sing along, rather than alone.

Oktoberfest: Best of the Wurst and Some Good Beer to Boot

It's a bit chilly outside, and the leaves are turning. The kids are into the swing of school and the buses rumble by at the same time, morning and evening. Winter isn't here yet, but October is, and not everyone in town is German, but that never stopped anyone from heading to Oktoberfest. There's nothing quite like it, a big ol' tent full of people you never met before but now they feel like family, and there's a polka band playing and good food piled high. Seems like something we can do ourselves right here at home. It's not too late to get out the grill, put some beer in a cooler, throw a few brats on, and whoop it on up.

Reuben Soup

German Short Ribs

Spaetzle

Reuben Potato Pizza

Hot German Potato Salad

Reuben Loaf

Grandma's Apple Slices

~ A FEW GOOD IDEAS FOR THE EVENING ~

DECOR . . . .

If the weather is amenable, turn your garage into a mini version of the real Oktoberfest. Give it a sweep, cover a few picnic tables with blue-and-white tablecloths, and shop for beer steins your guests can take home as a souvenir.

TO KEEP THE CONVERSATION GOING . . . .

You might teach your guests a little German. *Gemütlichkeit* (ge-moot-lick-kite) means "a state of comfort, belonging or coziness." This is what a good get-together should be like. Another fine word is *Schnapsidee* (shh-nops-i-day), which means, literally, a "schnapps idea." You know those times you've had a drink or two and entertained a crazy idea, like, "I know. Let's buy a Winnebago and head to Canada next week!" That would be a Schnapsidee.

SOMETHING TO DO . . . .

Polka. Unless you've inherited a few polka albums, pick up a few CDs of good polka music. And if, by chance, you know someone who plays the accordion, put 'em on the guest list.

WHAT TO DRINK . . . .

Suggest that your guests each bring their favorite autumn beer. I'm told the official Oktoberfest has six official beers, and you can find them around here: Augustiner, Hacker Pschorr, Hofbräu, Spaten, Löwenbräu and Paulaner. And for those who don't partake, no worries. It's not the beer; it's the camaraderie. A few bottles of sparkling apple cider will round it out nicely.

MAKE IT YOUR OWN . . . .

Host a "Best of the Wurst" contest. Challenge your guests to arrive with the most unique, delicious bratwurst they can find, or make. Apple brats, wild rice brats, blueberry brats. Have a brat tasting hour, and vote on the Very Best Brat. (I won last year with Gummy Bear brats. Seriously.)

Reuben Soup

½ cup chopped onions
½ cup sliced celery
2 T butter
1 cup chicken broth
1 cup beef broth
½ tsp baking soda
2 T cornstarch

2 T water
¾ cup sauerkraut, rinsed and drained
2 cup light cream
2 cup chopped, cooked corned beef
1 cup shredded Swiss cheese
Salt and pepper, to taste
Rye croutons, optional

In a large saucepan, sauté onion and celery in butter until tender. Add broths and baking soda. Combine cornstarch and water; add to pan. Bring to a boil; boil for 2 minutes, stirring occasionally. Reduce heat. Add sauerkraut, cream and corned beef; simmer for 15 minutes. Add cheese; heat until melted. Add salt and pepper.

Garnish with croutons.

German Short Ribs

6 T flour, divided
1 tsp salt
⅛ tsp ground black pepper
3 lbs boneless beef short ribs
2 T olive oil
1 onion, sliced
1 cup dry red wine

1 cup chili sauce
6 T packed brown sugar
6 T vinegar
2 T Worcestershire sauce
1 tsp dry mustard
1 tsp chili powder
½ cup water

In a small bowl, combine 2 T flour, salt and pepper. Coat the short ribs with the flour mixture.

In a large skillet, brown the short ribs in the olive oil over medium-high heat. (Do not fully cook them yet.) In a slow cooker, combine onion, wine, chili sauce, brown sugar, vinegar, Worcestershire sauce, mustard and chili powder. Mix thoroughly. Transfer the short ribs from the skillet to the slow cooker. Cover, and cook on low for 6 to 8 hours.

Remove ribs and turn the slow cooker to high. Mix the remaining 4 T of flour with ½ cup water and stir into sauce. Cook for 10 minutes or until slightly thickened.

(Note: Boneless beef short ribs can actually be pretty tough to find, but yes, they actually do exist.)

Spaetzle

4 cups all-purpose flour
2 tsp salt
2 tsp ground nutmeg
3-4 dashes white pepper
8 eggs, lightly beaten

1 cup milk
4 quarts chicken broth or water
4-8 T butter
Bowl of ice water
Grated Parmesan cheese, optional

Combine the flour, salt, nutmeg and pepper in a large bowl. Add eggs and milk, and mix well to a thick batter. In a Dutch oven or a large kettle, bring chicken broth to a boil. Drop batter by ½ teaspoonfuls into boiling liquid. Boil until spaetzle rises to the surface; remove to ice water. Drain well. In a large skillet, heat spaetzle in butter until lightly browned. Pour into serving dish and sprinkle with Parmesan.

Makes 8 servings.

Reuben Potato Pizza

3 to 4 medium potatoes, scrubbed
   and very thinly sliced
Kosher salt and black pepper
3 T cornstarch
3 to 4 T beef stock
Olive oil, for brushing, plus 1 T
2 T butter
1 medium onion, very finely chopped
4-5 cloves garlic, finely chopped

1 tsp paprika
½ to ¾ lb corned beef,
   very finely chopped
½ lb sauerkraut, drained and rinsed
2 cups shredded Gruyère cheese
½ cup sour cream
¼ cup ketchup
2 T pickle relish

Place potatoes in a large, shallow bowl or dish and season with salt and pepper; sprinkle with cornstarch.

Brush a large, 12-inch pizza pan liberally with olive oil. Arrange potatoes around pan, working all the way to edges and overlapping the slices evenly to form the potato crust. Press crust down to set then brush with olive oil; sprinkle with 1–2 T stock. Bake 15–20 minutes at 425, or until potatoes are cooked through.

In a skillet over medium heat, melt butter. Add onions and garlic, and season with a little salt, pepper and the paprika. Cook to tender, 7–8 minutes. Add corned beef and remaining beef stock, and cover. Cook until crispy on the bottom.

Top the potato crust with a thin layer of sauerkraut, then corned beef and cheese. Bake or broil in the lower third of the oven at 425 until nicely brown and bubbly. In a small mixing bowl, mix together the sour cream, ketchup and relish. Transfer to a squeeze bottle and squeeze onto top of pizza, or dollop evenly around the pizza.

Hot German Potato Salad

6 medium potatoes (about 2 lbs)
1 tsp salt

In large saucepan, combine potatoes and salt in water. Cook until tender, about 25 minutes. Drain, let cool, and cut into thick slices.

Dressing

6 slices bacon
Vegetable oil
¼ cup cider vinegar
¼ cup water
1 tsp sugar

½ tsp salt
¼ tsp pepper
1 egg, slightly beaten
⅓ cup finely chopped green onion
2 T minced fresh parsley

In large skillet, cook bacon over medium heat until crisp. Drain on paper towels.

Measure bacon drippings; add oil to make ⅓ cup and pour back into skillet. Add vinegar, water, sugar, salt, pepper, egg and onion. Cook and stir over medium heat just until thickened. Crumble bacon and add to skillet with potatoes and 1 T parsley. Mix well and heat through. Garnish with remaining parsley.

Reuben Loaf

1 can of crescent rolls
½ lb of sliced corned beef
½ lb Swiss cheese
1 (14 oz) can sauerkraut, drained
8 oz tomato sauce
⅓ cup Thousand Island dressing

Mix together sauerkraut, tomato sauce and dressing.

In an 8x8 baking dish or cake pan, spread a layer of half the crescent roll dough and cover with half the cheese. Next, layer half of the meat, all of the sauce, the rest of the meat, then the rest of the cheese. Top it off with the other half of the dough.

Bake at 350 degrees for 20 to 30 minutes until the top is golden brown. Cool 10 minutes before serving.

Cut into squares.

Grandma's Apple Slices

2 eggs, separated
Milk
3 cups flour
2 T sugar
1 tsp salt
1 cup shortening
2 T butter

Corn flakes
7-8 cups peeled, sliced apples
1 cup sugar
2-3 tsp cinnamon
Dashes of nutmeg

Place 2 egg yolks in glass measuring cup and set whites aside. Add milk to yolks to make ⅔ cup. Blend together flour, sugar, salt, shortening and butter. Add milk and yolk mixture, and combine well. Roll out ½ the dough to fit the bottom of a cookie sheet or two 9x13 cake pans. Crumble at least ½ cup corn flakes on the crust. Set aside.

Mix apples with sugar, cinnamon and nutmeg. Pour onto prepared crust and spread out evenly. Roll out remaining dough and place over top of apples. Seal edges.

Beat egg whites until fluffy, and spread over top crust. Bake at 400 until lightly brown. Frost with your favorite powdered sugar frosting, or serve plain with ice cream.

Enjoy!

HOW IT ALL WENT

Invited friends over on Saturday, and it was a good time. Mr. Sundberg spent the morning getting the garage ready, and I spent most of my time making potato salad, spaetzle and apple slice bars. I'd left the German chocolate cake to Mr. Ableidinger, as it's his specialty.

I laid Mr. Sundberg's lederhosen and his alpine hat out on the bed just in case he felt compelled to put 'em on. They were a gift from friends who visited Germany, and my gift was a Dirndl and apron and frilly blouse (think St. Pauli Girl, almost) and I wore it and felt silly only for a while.

Wasn't long before we found ourselves in the garage together, sipping beer and tasting brats, and everyone loved the corned beef hash potato pie Mrs. Lund made, and my spaetzle was a hit. The Best of the Wurst went to the Hansens, who brought cranberry spice brats that were out of this world, and Mr. Ableidinger made not one but two German chocolate cakes, with coconut caramel frosting a mile high. Mr. Sundberg disappeared sometime during dessert, and suddenly there was polka music, and there he was, lederhosen, alpine hat and hand extended to me. "Will you dance?" he asked, and everyone cheered, and I felt myself blushing. I nodded, took his hand, and danced with him, bless his Scandinavian heart. "You look lovely, my dear," he whispered, and we danced to "The Beer Barrel Polka."

Harvest Dinner

They say too much of a good thing is not such a good thing, but this time of year it's not possible. There's food in abundance from gardens and farms, and we've all worked hard through a long, hot summer. Seems meet, right and salutary to gather together in gratitude for all we have, to partake in a feast, and to celebrate the good fortune of good food and good friends.

Pumpkin Dip

Winter Vegetable Stew

Apple Brown Sugar Pork Chops

Easy Crock Pot Scalloped Potatoes

Parmesan-Roasted Acorn Squash

Sweet Potato Bake

Spicy Baked Apples

Pumpkin Pie Squares

Carmel Apple Cheesecake

~ A FEW GOOD IDEAS FOR THE EVENING ~

DECOR . . . .

Use fresh fruit, small pumpkins, squash and gourds in a cornucopia-type centerpiece. Maybe a bale of hay or two outside the door, some wood piled up, and a pumpkin with the word "Harvest" carved in and lit up in the night.

TO KEEP THE CONVERSATION GOING . . . . . .

"What are you thankful for?" might be the question of the night. Or make it about the people at the table: one person is in the spotlight for a bit while each person at the table shares what they're thankful for about that person. Go 'round until everyone has expressed a kind sentiment about everyone else.

SOMETHING TO DO . . . .

Bobbing for apples may be old school, but it sure can be fun. And you're never too old for pumpkin carving. Consider dividing up in teams for larger pumpkins, or supply smaller pumpkins, one per person. You might suggest a pumpkin carving contest. And the prizes? Caramel apples rolled in crushed nuts, mini-apple pies, or half a peck of apples.

WHAT TO DRINK . . . .

Pick up a jug of apple cider from the orchard, and make a batch of hot, buttered apple cider mix. Cream together a pound of dark brown sugar with half a cup of butter. Add a teaspoon of cinnamon, half a teaspoon of cloves and a quarter teaspoon of ground nutmeg. Mix it all together, and chill. When you're ready to serve, place a big heaping tablespoon of the mix in a mug, and fill the mug with simmering hot cider.

MAKE IT YOUR OWN . . . .

Invite everyone to bring a sack of food for the food shelf, or create a "meal" to deliver to a shelter. Play some classical music through the evening— Beethoven's "Ode to Joy" or maybe some cello music, there in the background.

Pumpkin Dip

1 (8 oz) package cream cheese, softened
2 cups pumpkin pie filling
2 cups powdered sugar
1 tsp ground cinnamon
¼ to ½ tsp ground ginger

Beat cream cheese in a large bowl until smooth. Beat in pumpkin pie filling. Add the sugar, cinnamon and ginger and mix well. Serve with cookies. Store leftover dip in the refrigerator.

Makes about 3 cups of dip.

Winter Vegetable Stew

1 medium parsnip, peeled and
    cut into ¼-inch cubes
1 medium boiling or Yukon Gold
    potato, peeled and cut into
    ½-inch cubes
5 cups water
½ cup soy sauce
1 T onion powder
¼ cup Guinness or other stout beer
2 T Worcestershire sauce
4 T butter
1 small yellow onion, finely chopped
1 carrot, peeled and thinly chopped
2 stalks celery, finely chopped
1 medium leek (white and pale green
    parts only), thinly sliced

½ cup flour
¼ cup nutritional yeast
1 tsp salt
½ tsp freshly ground black pepper
½ tsp dry mustard
Pinch of nutmeg
1 bay leaf
Pinch of fresh or dried sage
Pinch of fresh or dried rosemary
Pinch of fresh or dried thyme
½ cup corn, fresh or frozen
1 cup milk

Boil parsnip and potato in a blend of water, soy sauce, onion powder, beer and
Worcestershire sauce until barely tender; drain and set aside.

Melt butter in a large stockpot and add onion, carrot, celery and leek. Sauté
until vegetables are tender. Add flour, yeast, salt, black pepper, dry mustard,
nutmeg and herbs and cook over gentle heat for 5 minutes. Increase heat and
gradually stir in boiled parsnip and potato mixture. Simmer, stirring frequently,
for 10 to 15 minutes. Add corn and milk and simmer for 5 minutes. Remove bay
leaf. Serve immediately.

Makes 6 to 8 servings.

Apple Brown Sugar Pork Chops

4 pork chops (1 inch thick)

2 apples, sliced or chopped into small pieces

2 sticks of butter

1 cup brown sugar

Several dashes of cinnamon

In a large skillet, add 1½ sticks of butter and brown sugar. Cook the pork chop strips on medium heat until pork is cooked through. Once the pork starts looking done, add the rest of the butter and the apples until slightly softened but not limp. Serve with vegetables and potatoes, or noodles, even.

Easy Crock Pot Scalloped Potatoes

8-10 medium potatoes

8 oz of sour cream

1 can of mushroom soup (could use potato or cream of chicken soup)

1 T dehydrated onion

1 T Worcestershire sauce

1 to 2 oz bacon bits, store bought or home fried

8 oz finely shredded sharp cheddar cheese

Mix sour cream, soup, onion and Worcestershire in a large bowl. Thinly slice potatoes and add to mixture. (If potatoes are cut too thick the dish will take much longer to cook.) Spray crock pot with oil. Spread half of the potato mixture into crock pot. Sprinkle on bacon bits followed by cheese. Add second layer of potatoes. Finish with another layer of bacon bits and cheese. Cover and cook on high 4–7 hours, depending on crock pot.

Parmesan-Roasted Acorn Squash

1 (2 lbs) acorn squash, halved, seeded and sliced ¾ inch thick, leaving skin on
2 T olive oil
8 sprigs fresh thyme
½ tsp salt
½ tsp pepper
¼ cup grated Parmesan cheese

Heat oven to 400. On a rimmed baking sheet, toss the squash with the oil, thyme, salt and pepper. Sprinkle with the Parmesan. Roast the squash until golden brown and tender, 20–30 minutes, depending on your oven.

Serves 4.

Sweet Potato Bake

3 cans (15 oz) sweet potatoes, drained
¼ cup melted butter
2 tsp pumpkin pie spice
Dash nutmeg
3 cups mini-marshmallows

Mash potatoes, butter and spices in large bowl until blended. Scoop into greased 1½-quart casserole dish; top with marshmallows. Bake at 350 for 15–20 minutes, until potatoes are heated through and marshmallows are lightly browned.

Spicy Baked Apples

6 baking apples, medium- to large-sized
½ cup light brown sugar
½ cup cinnamon red hot candies
½ tsp cinnamon (I triple the cinnamon, but that's just me)

Do not peel the apples, as the skin helps them hold their shape when baking. Do slice off and set aside the very top of the apples. Core the apples, leaving a good half inch at the bottom. Arrange in an 8x8 buttered baking dish.

In a small bowl, combine brown sugar, cinnamon red hots and cinnamon. Fill each apple with the mixture. Replace the apple tops and sprinkle the remaining mixture over.

Bake at 350, uncovered, for 30 minutes, or until apples are tender. Baste with pan sauce and bake another 15 minutes or so, basting occasionally. Serve hot or cold with pan sauce spooned over apples.

Pumpkin Pie Squares

Crust

 1 cup flour
 ½ cup oatmeal
 ½ cup brown sugar
 1 stick butter, softened

Cut together in lightly greased 9x13 pan until crumbly. Press flat.
Bake 15 minutes at 350.

Filling

 1 (15 oz) can of pumpkin
 1 (13½ oz) can evaporated milk
 2 eggs
 ¾ cup sugar
 ½ tsp salt
 ½ tsp cinnamon (I throw in a bit more)
 ½ tsp ginger
 ½ tsp cloves

Whisk together until blended. Pour over cooled crust. Bake at 350 for
20 minutes or so, until center is no longer wobbly.

Let cool a bit, and serve with Cool Whip or ice cream. Or cool completely,
cut into bars, and refrigerate.

Caramel Apple Cheesecake

2 cups crushed graham crackers
¼ cup sugar
1 stick butter, melted
2 (8 oz) blocks cream cheese, softened
4 cups powdered sugar
12 oz Cool Whip
2-3 red and/or green apples, diced
Your favorite caramel sauce

Mix first three ingredients and press into a 9x13 cake pan. Chill.

Cream together cream cheese and powdered sugar, and fold in Cool Whip. Spread over crust. Refrigerate an hour or two.

Top with diced apple, and drizzle caramel sauce over.

Enjoy!

HOW IT ALL WENT

Invited some friends over Saturday, and it was a good time. No snow yet, but there's a real chill in the air, and the coats on the bench were piled high. Our friends each came with food for dinner and for the food shelf, and there were seven bottles of wine to go into the fridge. Everyone wore sweaters and had red cheeks, and the kitchen was bustling.

It's not often we take time to express gratitude, and that's what we did Saturday night. It was humbling, really, to hear our friends share with each other those things for which they are grateful. Mr. Hansen thanked Mr. Lund for teaching him about patience, and Mrs. Stendahl told Mr. Stendahl that she admires his persistence. Mr. Sundberg was quiet, and when he spoke, it was brief. He told us all that his life is richer for our presence, and that he's grateful to be blessed with such friends. I had tears in my eyes more than once, especially when Mrs. Lund said if it weren't for me, she'd never have considered baking a pie, and that was something to hear. Especially since she makes the best peach pie in the county.

Instead of bobbing for apples, we stayed at the table and ate cheesecake and played Swedish Rummy. We talked about our plans and when we might next meet, and I think that was the latest our friends have ever stayed. It was after midnight and there we were at the table, content in every way, and happy to play just one more round.

Soups, Stews and Comfort Food

When the snow comes before we expect it to, it can be a bit disconcerting. Don't get me wrong—I love snow. I love storms and thunder and driving winds. I love the sparkle of sun on the morning drifts and the quiet of big flakes falling and how trees look after a storm. I love getting supplies and being trapped in my house for three days and making snowmen. I get some real satisfaction out of shoveling, but what I love as much is coming in from a few hours out in the cold and cooking for friends coming over to relax for an evening.

Cheese Soup

Bacon Corn Chowder

White Chicken Chili

Three Cheese Onion Comfort Soup

Dang Good Beef Stew

Easy Crock Pot Potato Soup

Cheesy Garlic Biscuits

Pumpkin Cornbread

Mrs. Sundberg's Mother's Pretty Good Apple Pie

~ A FEW GOOD IDEAS FOR THE EVENING ~

DECOR . . . .

Make a corn husk centerpiece, and light a few candles. Set bowls of candy corn here and there, or homemade caramels. Nothing complicated or fancy, though you might find out your guests' favorite sweets ahead of time and make sure they're within reach.

TO KEEP THE CONVERSATION GOING . . . .

During dinner, ask, "What was the best meal you ever had?" Or, "If you could plan your last meal, what would it be?"

SOMETHING TO DO . . . .

Ask guests to bring a board game, old or new, a game that the group can play together. Gather in a living room or family room where people can sit on the floor, and lounge a bit.

WHAT TO DRINK . . . .

Again, keep it simple, as the idea is to relax. Invite guests to bring a bottle of what they feel is a "comfort drink," like Baileys Irish Cream, or Grand Marnier. Offer up some hot chocolate made with milk.

MAKE IT YOUR OWN . . . .

Encourage guests to wear loose fitting clothing or pants with elastic waistbands. Pajamas, if they wish. You could have people each bring a crock pot of soup or stew, and make it a buffet. Provide a variety of spoons for people to use with their soups—some people prefer traditional, some small, some large. Place the spoons in glass spoon jars in the middle of the table. And rather than cut the bread, encourage people to break off a chunk and pass the loaf around.

Cheese Soup

¼ cup chopped onion
1 T butter
½ cup celery
½ cup chopped carrots
3 cups potatoes, peeled and chopped
1 tsp parsley
1 chicken bouillon cube
½ tsp salt
1-2 cups water
1½ cups milk
2 T flour
½ lb medium cheddar or Velveeta cheese
Pepper, to taste

In your favorite stockpot, sauté onions in butter for a few minutes until onions start to become clear. Add celery and carrots, and stir fry another few minutes. Add potatoes, parsley, bouillon cube and salt, and enough water to just cover the vegetables. Simmer 10 minutes or so, or until veggies are soft.

Add milk, flour and cheese, and a bit of pepper. Cook on low, stirring occasionally, until cheese is melted. Garnish with popcorn.

Bacon Corn Chowder

4 bacon slices
½ cup refrigerated pre-chopped celery, onion and bell pepper mix
2 (16 oz) packages frozen baby gold and white corn, thawed, divided
2 cups milk, divided
½ tsp salt
¼ tsp freshly ground black pepper
¾ cup (3 oz) extra-sharp cheddar cheese
Freshly ground black pepper (optional)

Cook bacon in a Dutch oven over medium heat until crisp. Remove bacon from pan; crumble and set aside. Add celery mixture and 1 package corn to drippings in pan; sauté 5 minutes or until vegetables are tender.

Place remaining 1 package corn and 1 cup milk in a blender, and process until smooth. Add pureed mixture to vegetables in pan; stir in remaining 1 cup milk, salt, black pepper and cheese. Cook over medium heat (do not boil), stirring constantly, until cheese melts. Ladle chowder into bowls. Top each serving evenly with crumbled bacon. Sprinkle with additional black pepper, if desired.

White Chicken Chili

1 tsp of lemon pepper seasoning (or lime pepper if you have it)

2 tsp of ground cumin

2½ cups of chicken stock

4 chopped cooked chicken breasts (I also add some dark meat)

2 or more cloves (to taste) garlic, chopped

2 cups chopped onion

2 (8 oz) cans of white shoepeg corn, drained

2 large (15 oz) cans of hominy (often found in the Mexican food section of the grocery)

2 (4 oz) cans of chopped green chiles, undrained. (you could substitute 1 can of jalapeño chiles, if preferred)

2 to 4 (14 oz) cans of great northern beans, undrained.

Juice of half a lime

In stockpot, combine seasonings, broth, chicken and simmer. Add garlic, onion, corn, hominy, green chiles and continue to simmer. Add beans and fresh lime juice last, and simmer for another 45 minutes.

Garnish with shredded Monterey Jack or Colby-Jack, cilantro, sour cream and/ or jalapeño slices.

Serves about 8.

Three Cheese Onion Comfort Soup

¾ stick butter
3 medium onions, sliced
3 (14.5 oz) cans broth
1½ broth cans of water
2 tsp Worcestershire sauce
½ tsp garlic powder
⅛ tsp cayenne pepper
Croutons
Parmesan cheese
Swiss cheese
Mozzarella cheese

Melt butter in 2½-quart pot. Add sliced onions and cook for 30 minutes or so, stirring occasionally. Add broth, water, Worcestershire sauce, garlic powder and cayenne pepper. Cook 30 more minutes, stirring now and then. Pour into individual soup bowls, top with croutons, sprinkle with Parmesan cheese, slice of Swiss and slice of mozzarella. Microwave until cheese is melted, or broil in oven on foil-covered cookie sheet. Serve with fresh fruit, more bread, and some kind of gooey brownie.

Dang Good Beef Stew

¼ cup all-purpose flour
2 pounds boneless beef chuck roast, trimmed and cut into 1-inch cubes
2 T oil
1 can (10.75 oz) condensed tomato soup
1 cup water or red wine
2 beef bouillon cubes
3 tsp Italian seasoning
1 bay leaf
½ tsp coarsely ground pepper
6 white onions or yellow onions, quartered
4 medium potatoes, cut into 1½-inch slices
3 medium carrots, cut into 1-inch slices
12 large fresh mushrooms
½ cup sliced celery

Place flour in a large resealable plastic bag. Add beef, a few pieces at a time, and shake to coat. In a large skillet, brown meat in oil in batches; drain. Transfer to a 5-quart slow cooker. Combine the tomato soup, water or wine, bouillon, Italian seasoning, bay leaf and pepper; pour over beef. Add the onions, potatoes, carrots, mushrooms and celery. Cover and cook on low for 4 to 5 hours or until meat is tender. Discard bay leaf.

Easy Crock Pot Potato Soup

  1 (30 oz) bag of frozen diced hash browns
  32 oz chicken broth (the boxed ones work great)
  1 (10 oz) can of cream of chicken soup
  4 oz bacon bits
  Salt and pepper, to taste
  1 (8 oz) package cream cheese
  1 cup shredded cheddar cheese

Put the potatoes in the crock pot, and add the chicken broth, cream of chicken soup and half of the bacon bits. Add a pinch of salt and pepper.

Cook on low for 8 hours or until potatoes are tender. An hour before serving, cut the cream cheese into small cubes. Place the cubes in the crock pot. Mix a few times throughout the hour before serving. Once the cream cheese is completely mixed in, it's ready to serve.

Top with cheddar cheese and some additional bacon bits.

Cheesy Garlic Biscuits

2 cups Bisquick or similar baking mix
⅔ cup milk
½ cup grated sharp cheddar cheese
½ cup melted butter
¼ tsp garlic salt

Mix Bisquick, milk and cheddar until a soft ball forms. Beat vigorously for 30 seconds. Drop by balls onto an ungreased baking sheet and bake at 450 degrees for 8 to 10 minutes. Mix butter and garlic salt and brush on rolls while still hot on the pan.

Pumpkin Cornbread

2 cups cornmeal
2 cups flour
1 cup sugar
2 T baking powder
½ tsp baking soda
4 eggs
1 cup vegetable oil
2¼ cups pureed pumpkin
1 cup milk

Combine all the dry ingredients in a large bowl. Beat together the eggs, oil, pumpkin, and milk. Fold the wet ingredients into the dry with a rubber spatula. The batter will be smooth and fluffy.

Pour the batter into a 9x13 baking pan (or two loaf pans), and place in the middle rack of the oven. Bake for 25 minutes at 350, or until a toothpick stuck in the middle of the cornbread comes out dry. Let cool for 10 minutes, and then cut and serve.

Mrs. Sundberg's Mother's Pretty Good Apple Pie

7-8 tart apples (the family favorite—sweet, tart or a combo)
Just short of 1 cup sugar
2 T flour
1 tsp cinnamon
A pinch of nutmeg (I use 2 or 3)
A dash of salt
Pastry for double-crust 9-inch pie
2 T butter

Pare apples and slice thin. Combine sugar, flour, spices and salt; mix with apples. Line 9-inch pie plate with pastry and fill with apple mixture; dot with butter. Adjust top crust and crimp edges. Brush lightly with milk, or the juice from the filling mixture, and sprinkle with sugar for sparkle. Bake at 375 to 400, 50 minutes or 'til done.

Enjoy!

HOW IT ALL WENT

Invited friends over Saturday, and it was a good time. I knew the snow was coming and I figured, why not invite some people over and meet it head-on with an evening inside eating beef stew and playing games?

I knew I'd have to plan some time to clear a path. Didn't take long at all. People ask why we don't have a snowblower, and it's a good question, given where we live. Thing is, we have a big snow only two or three times a winter, and Mr. S. and I usually have the time and energy to shovel it. There are financial concerns, too, and the fact that friendly neighbors have offered to snowblow our drive now and then. It seems so much of life is automated these days that a person can get by without working much at all, and I don't think that's all good.

The evening was low-key, simple and fun. Everyone brought bread, and we ate cheese soup and beef stew and white chicken chili, and afterward lit the fire and played Scrabble and Yahtzee and ended with Monopoly. All the men wore plaid flannel pajama bottoms, and Mrs. Stendahl wore blue footie pajamas, and Mrs. Hansen wore purple sweatpants and a matching sweatshirt. I'm most comfortable in jeans and one of Mr. Sundberg's flannel shirts, so that's what I wore. As we were eating apple pie, someone said, "Look, it's snowing again!" And it was. And I smiled.

Home Is the Hunter

"Home is the sailor, / home from the sea, / And the hunter home from the hill." Not sure where I first read the poem, or when, but I always think of those lines when hunting season rolls around. Not everyone's a fan of venison, but cook it right and your friends who have never tried it will be glad they did. And they'll ask you for the recipe. Wait and see.

Creamed Pheasant on Rice

Good Rice

Hearty Venison Stew

Venison Chops

Sliced Baked Potatoes

Blueberry Wild Rice Muffins

Cream Cheese Frosted Carrot Cake

~ A FEW GOOD IDEAS FOR THE EVENING ~

DECOR . . . .

Use orange camo for a table cloth. You can find camouflage party supplies at lots of stores. Hang a rack of horns or a mounted deer head, if you want to go all out. And guests ought to come wearing at least one article of camo clothing.

TO KEEP THE CONVERSATION GOING . . . .

Share hunting stories. Of all sorts, either your own hunting story or one you heard. To include hunters and non-hunters alike, and it doesn't have to involve a rifle, talk about a time you looked for something and found it. Anything goes.

SOMETHING TO DO . . . .

Let people know to bring warm clothes, and set up a few hay bales out back, complete with a target. Invite any archers in the group to prepare an archery lesson, and shoot a few arrows before dinner. You may be surprised—often the people least interested at the start end up being the ones most reluctant to stop. Or plan a scavenger hunt in the forest or fields nearby.

WHAT TO DRINK . . . .

Buy a couple growlers of beer for the fridge. Whiskey on ice is good, too, and so are whiskey sours. Or just beer. Home-brewed beer would be a nice touch.

MAKE IT YOUR OWN . . . .

If you've got what you need and the mood is right, have a go at Big Buck Hunter, the video game. Or read aloud Richard Connell's short story, published in 1924, "The Most Dangerous Game." Everyone likes to be read to, and this one's a humdinger.

Creamed Pheasant on Rice

1 pheasant (serves four people)
2-3 T flour (more if you run out)
½ tsp salt
½ tsp pepper
2 T butter
1 cup water
1-2 T chopped onion

1 stalk celery, diced
4 oz sliced fresh mushrooms
1 (10.75 oz) can cream of mushroom
   or cream of chicken soup
2-3 T milk or cream
Salt and pepper, to taste

Fillet meat off breast of pheasant (or cut in half lengthwise). Remove thighs from leg by disjointing at knee. Remove all shot and feathers from meat.

Shake meat pieces in paper bag with 2–3 T flour and salt and pepper. Brown meat pieces in butter in skillet. When brown, add 1 cup water, cover, and simmer meat until thighs are tender—about 30 to 45 min.

When tender, remove meat from skillet, and take out any remaining bones. Cut meat into bite-sized pieces. Add 1 T chopped onion to remaining juice in skillet, along with celery and simmer a few minutes. Add 4 oz sliced fresh mushrooms. Add water if needed, and simmer a few minutes more. Add 1 can cream of mushroom or cream of chicken soup, and meat. Stir, and add enough milk (or add some cream if you feel decadent) to reach desired consistency. Season to taste. Simmer half an hour or so on low heat.

Serve over a mix of wild rice and white rice (recipe on next page).

Good Rice

¼ cup wild rice
2½ cups chicken broth, divided
1 T butter
¾ cup white rice

Simmer wild rice in 1 cup chicken broth and 1 T butter, covered, for 40 minutes.
Add white rice and 1½ cups broth. Cover and simmer another 20 minutes.
Add a bit of water to rice if rice seems dry. Remove from heat and let rice
stand, covered, 5–10 minutes. Serve creamed pheasant over the rice. You can
embellish with veggies, your own favorite seasonings and your choice of wine.

Hearty Venison Stew

1 to 1½ lbs lean beef (or venison) cut into ¾- to 1-inch cubes

2 T flour

Salt and pepper

2 T cooking oil

2 T minced onion

2 beef bouillon cubes

¼ tsp garlic powder

½ tsp dried thyme leaves

½ tsp dried basil

1 bay leaf

1 (8 oz) can tomato sauce

3-4 medium carrots, peeled and chunked

3 large stalks of celery, chopped into small chunks

About 3 cups peeled potatoes, cut into cubes (if reds, you don't have to peel 'em)

1-2 small shots of Tabasco or ⅛ tsp cayenne pepper (if desired)

Shake meat in paper bag with flour and a little salt and pepper. Brown over high heat in oil, stirring frequently. Add onion near end of browning. Turn heat down to low, just barely cover meat with water, and add bouillon, garlic powder, thyme, basil and bay leaf. Simmer in covered pot ½ hour or so (more if meat is tough). Add tomato sauce. Stir occasionally. When meat is just about tender enough, add carrots, celery and potatoes, in that order, at about 1- to 2-minute intervals. Simmer further until vegetables are tender, adding more water, if needed, just to keep covered. Stir occasionally, checking for doneness of vegetables. Add Tabasco or cayenne, and more salt and pepper, to taste, if needed. Serve in a stew bowl with fresh dinner rolls or a good, dense bread. Because stew is an art form, no two should turn out exactly alike.

Venison Chops

4-6 venison chops
Vegetable oil
Butter
1 to 2 cups flour
Salt and pepper
½ to ¾ cup brown sugar
2 to 3 T ketchup
½ medium onion, minced
1 T basil
2 to 3 T butter
1 cup beef broth, more if desired
Pepper, to taste

Pound the chops until they are ¼ inch or so thick. In a large skillet, heat oil and butter (2 T oil to 1 T butter) over medium heat. Place 1–2 cups flour in a bowl, adding a few shakes each of salt and pepper. Dredge the chops in the mixture and place in heated skillet. Brown on both sides. Place chops in a 9x13 cake pan, and continue until all the chops are browned, adding more oil and butter as needed. Sprinkle brown sugar over all of the browned chops, squirt a dab of ketchup on each, and top with minced onion. Sprinkle basil over all of it, and dot each chop with butter. Pour beef broth into the pan and cover with foil. Bake at 350 for 1 hour and 15 minutes or until done.

Sliced Baked Potatoes

4 medium baking potatoes (evenly sized)
1 tsp salt
2-3 T melted butter
2-3 T chopped fresh herbs (parsley, chives, thyme, sage)
 or 2-3 tsp dried herbs, your choice
4-6 T grated cheddar cheese
1½ T Parmesan cheese

Scrub and rinse potatoes, and cut into thin slices, but don't cut all the way through. It helps to place the handle of a spoon or a table knife alongside the potato to prevent the knife from slicing through.

Place cut potatoes in a baking dish, and gently fan out the slices.

Sprinkle with salt, drizzle with butter, and sprinkle with herbs.

Bake potatoes at 425 for about 50 minutes. Remove from oven and sprinkle with cheeses.

Bake potatoes another 10 to 15 minutes until lightly browned, cheeses are melted and potatoes are soft inside. Check for doneness with a fork or skewer.

Blueberry Wild Rice Muffins

1 cup fully cooked wild rice
2 eggs, beaten
⅓ cup oil
⅓ cup honey or brown sugar
¾ cup buttermilk
¼ cup sour cream
2½ cups flour
4 tsp baking powder
½ tsp salt
1 cup blueberries

In medium bowl, mix rice, eggs, oil, honey (or brown sugar), buttermilk and sour cream. In large bowl, mix flour, baking powder and salt. Stir in blueberries. Add ingredients from medium bowl into large bowl, stirring until just blended. Spoon into prepared muffin tins. Sprinkle lightly with sugar. Bake at 425 degrees for 15 to 18 minutes. Makes 18 muffins.

Cream Cheese Frosted Carrot Cake

1½ cups vegetable oil
4 eggs
3 cups raw shredded carrots
2 cups flour
2 tsp soda
2 tsp cinnamon
1 cup chopped walnuts
1 tsp salt

Frosting

8 oz cream cheese
1 stick butter
2 tsp vanilla
1 lb powdered sugar

Mix together all cake ingredients and bake in a lightly greased 9x13 cake pan at 350 for 45–60 minutes.

For frosting, cream together cream cheese, butter and vanilla. Slowly blend in powdered sugar. Frost cake when cool.

Enjoy!

HOW IT ALL WENT

Invited some friends over Saturday, and it was good time. It was my idea, really, to host a hunter's dinner. I grew up with hunters all 'round, and even though I don't hunt much myself, a lot of people I know and love spend a week or two this time of year out in the woods. I think there's more to it all than shooting a deer, really. One might compare it to shopping or baking—there's something to the endeavor itself. Doesn't matter if you come home empty-handed, or the cake doesn't turn out.

Lot of hunting stories got told Saturday night. Mr. Ableidinger only hunts pheasant, and both the Stendahls hunt grouse. On occasion, Mr. Sundberg takes his gun with him when walking in the woods, but he never brings anything home. The Hansens are hikers, and hunting makes them a bit tense, but Mr. Lund is a deer hunter, and he told us all about the big buck he shot last year. He'd hunted his whole life for that deer, and sure, he'll hunt some more, but he can relax now that he got his trophy deer.

He took us outside and showed us how to shoot a bow and arrow. On my third try, I launched an arrow and hit the edge of the target. I felt an odd rush of joy. I could get into this, I told him. And then I remembered the potatoes and took off into the house. Just in time, and was it ever good. Thinking I might ask for a bow and arrow for Christmas. Just for something new to try. Never do know.

Seafood, Fish and Some Time on the Lake

When you live where I live, you don't have to go far to find a lake, and with so many lakes around it would be a darn shame to let a winter go by without a little ice fishing expedition. We don't have an ice house, so it's overturned five-gallon buckets for us and Mr. Sundberg's hand auger to get through the ice. Ice fishing is a relaxing way to spend an afternoon, but can be a real hoot if you can make it a group outing and head home afterward to fry up your catch.

Scallop Chowder

Seafood Casserole

Broiled Walleye

Shrimp Scampi

Pan Fried Lake Fish

Fried Potatoes

Bacon Fried Green Beans

Fruit Crisp

~ A FEW GOOD IDEAS FOR THE EVENING ~

DECOR . . . .

If you've got a pet fish, make it a centerpiece. If not, run some fishing line here and there over the table and hang up some old lures. Create a bulletin board display of photos of friends and family out fishing, and holding up their northern and walleye and perch. Lean a fishing pole up against the toilet, just for fun.

TO KEEP THE CONVERSATION GOING . . . .

Tell fishing stories. Have each person share a story, anything having to do with fishing. Stories about the strangest thing you've caught are always good.

SOMETHING TO DO . . . .

Spend the afternoon ice fishing at a nearby lake. If anyone has never ice fished before, invite the more experienced people in the group to offer up some tips. Ice fishing is like anything else; people who try it often get hooked.

Or create an ice fishing trivia game with questions like, "How thick does the ice have to be before you can drive on it?" and "What is the most common lure used in ice fishin'?" (Answer: Swedish pimple. Though I prefer teardrops with waxies or a Flirty Girty, and I've heard chicken skin works well.) "Do you use a skimmer, chisel, pick or a gaff to clear slush from the hole?" Give lures or fish-themed Christmas ornaments for prizes.

WHAT TO DRINK . . . .

Hot chocolate, hot chocolate, hot chocolate. Request that guests bring their favorite hot chocolate mix. Have some amaretto on hand to spice it up.

MAKE IT YOUR OWN . . . .

Invite people to eat with their hands when necessary. Provide wetnaps, and even personalized bibs. If you're serving mixed drinks, make ice cubes ahead of time, and slip a gummy worm in each one. Or a Swedish fish.

Scallop Chowder

3 cups chicken broth
1 carrot, chopped
1 stalk celery, chopped
1 onion, chopped
3 potatoes, cubed
½ tsp thyme
2 T parsley
½ tsp salt
¼ tsp pepper
2 T butter
1 lb fresh mushrooms, sliced
1 lb scallops
½ cup white wine
1 egg yolk
1 cup heavy whipping cream

In a large pot over high heat, combine chicken broth, carrot, celery, onion, potatoes, thyme, parsley, salt and pepper, and bring to a boil. Reduce heat to medium-low and simmer for 10 to 15 minutes. Transfer mixture to a food processor or a blender and puree until smooth and set aside.

In the same pot over medium heat, sauté the mushrooms and scallops in the butter for 2 to 3 minutes. Add the wine and puree mixture to the pot, reduce heat to low and allow to simmer. In a separate small bowl, combine the egg yolk and heavy cream. Mix well and add to the soup. Continue simmering over low heat, stirring occasionally for 10 to 15 minutes.

Seafood Casserole

- 1 package (6 oz) long grain white rice and wild rice
- 1 pound cooked medium shrimp, peeled, deveined and cut into ½-inch pieces
- 1 pound frozen crab meat, thawed, or 2½ cups canned lump crab meat, drained
- 2 smaller celery stalks, chopped
- 1 medium onion, finely chopped
- ½ cup finely chopped green pepper
- 1 can (4 oz) mushroom stems and pieces, drained (fresh baby bellas, browned lightly in butter, are good, too)
- 1 jar (2 oz) diced pimientos, drained
- 1 cup mayo
- 1 cup milk, 2 percent or whole
- ½ tsp pepper
- Dash or two Worcestershire sauce
- ¼ cup dry breadcrumbs
- Salt and pepper, to taste

Cook rice according to directions on the package. In a large bowl, combine the shrimp, crab, celery, onion, green pepper, mushrooms and pimientos. Whisk together in a small bowl the mayo, milk, pepper and Worcestershire sauce; stir into seafood mixture. Add rice and mix well. Pour into a greased 13x9 baking dish. Sprinkle with breadcrumbs, salt and pepper. Bake uncovered at 375, 40–50 minutes or until bubbly.

Serves 4–6.

Broiled Walleye

⅓ cup sliced almonds, crushed
2 tsp lemon juice
1 T prepared mustard
1 T soy sauce
1 tsp sugar
Dash of red pepper
¼ cup heavy cream
4 walleye fillets (about 1½ lb)

Mix all ingredients (except fillets) and spread evenly over walleye fillets. Place fillets on a greased broiler pan and broil five inches from the heat in a preheated broiler for about 10 minutes, or until the fish flakes when probed with a fork.

Serves 4.

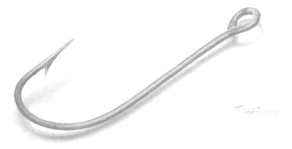

Shrimp Scampi

2 lb raw shrimp, peeled and deveined (tails optional)
1 cup olive oil
½ cup white whine
1 T oregano,
2 cloves garlic, crushed
1 T butter
1 lb spinach fettuccine, cooked

Combine first five ingredients in a bowl and cover. Marinade in refrigerator for 4 to 6 hours. Using a slotted spoon, remove shrimp and transfer to a fry pan, and sauté in 1 T butter, turning shrimp until they just turn pink. Do not overdo or shrimp will be tough.

Serve over buttered green spinach fettuccine. Serve with a nice white wine of your choice, maybe a Pinot Grigio, and a dense Italian or sourdough bread, with a side dish of herbed olive oil for dipping.

Serves 6.

Pan Fried Lake Fish

Fish fillets (bluegill, perch, sunfish or crappie)
Flour
Cornmeal
¼ tsp salt
Dash of pepper
Pinch of cayenne pepper
1 egg
½ cup milk
¼ cup oil, more if necessary

Pat thawed or fresh fillets dry with a paper towel. Place equal parts flour and cornmeal in a large Ziploc bag. Add salt, a dash of pepper, and an optional pinch of cayenne.

In a shallow dish, mix egg and milk well. Dredge fillets in egg mixture, and drop into bag of cornmeal and flour, 2–3 at a time. Seal and shake well.

In large skillet (cast iron preferably), heat ¼ cup oil to 375, or just starting to smoke. Lay fillets in skillet and fry 1–2 minutes on each side until lightly browned. Add more oil as needed. Remove to a platter covered with paper towels.

Serve with lemon wedges.

Fried Potatoes

5-6 potatoes
1-2 strips bacon, chopped
1 T oil

2 T chopped onion
Salt and pepper, to taste

Peel potatoes, or leave them unpeeled and simply wash. Slice lengthwise into four pieces. Put in a pot and cover with water. Bring to a boil; boil 10 minutes. Drain, and set aside to cool.

In a large skillet, place chopped bacon and oil. Stir-fry bacon until it simmers, and add onion. Stir and fry until bacon is done and onions begin to brown. Slice potatoes into bite-sized pieces; add and stir until potatoes begin to brown. Salt and pepper, to taste.

Bacon Fried Green Beans

Green beans, one handful per person
1-2 strips bacon, chopped
1 T oil

2 T chopped onion
Salt and pepper, to taste
¼ cup almond slivers, toasted

Snap ends off beans and wash. Bring water to boil in a pot, and add beans. Cover and bring to a boil; boil 18–20 minutes or until tender but not mushy. Drain and set aside.

In a large skillet, place chopped bacon and oil. Stir-fry bacon until it simmers, and add onion. Stir and fry until bacon is done and onions begin to brown. Add beans and stir-fry a minute or two. Salt and pepper, to taste.

Fruit Crisp

5 cups fruit
2-4 T sugar
½ cup rolled oats
½ cup brown sugar
¼ cup flour
¼ tsp ground nutmeg, ginger or cinnamon, depending on the fruit
¼ cup butter
¼ cup chopped nuts or coconut

Place fruit in a lightly greased 8x8 pan. Toss gently with sugar. Set aside.

In a medium bowl, mix together oats, sugar, flour and spice. Cut in butter. Stir in nuts or coconut.

Sprinkle mixture on top of the fruit and bake at 375 for 30–35 minutes.

For blueberry crisp, which can be tart, you may need to add an additional 4 T of sugar and 3 T of flour.

Enjoy!

HOW IT ALL WENT

Invited friends over Saturday, and it was a good time. It was my idea that we meet at the lake for some ice fishing, and was it ever fun. Everyone showed up wearing hats with earflaps, flannel shirts, snow pants and boots. We fished for nearly two hours, and pulled in a good number of perch, crappie and bluegill. Mr. Sundberg tried out his new Arctic Fisherman tip-ups, but Mr. Ableidinger had the most fun, I think. First time he's ever ice fished, and he caught the most fish of all. Every time he pulled one out of the lake, he hollered, "Woo hoo!" and we all clapped.

There's something about ice fishing, or maybe it's just being out on the lake, that brings out the kid in a person. Mrs. Lund and Mrs. Hansen both caught a good number of fish. Mrs. Lund, however, refused to remove the fish from the hook, and would swing it over to Mr. Lund or Mr. Hansen to remove it. The fourth or fifth fish she caught was a big ol' perch, and she heaved it up and swung it and whopped Mr. Lund on the face which sent everyone into a fit of laughter. Mrs. Hansen was laughing so hard, her bucket tipped over and she landed on the ice. Mr. Lund didn't flinch.

That meal of chowder, walleye, fried potatoes and green beans was one of the most satisfying dinners we've yet had together. Everyone was red-cheeked, all talking at once, and Mrs. Lund surprised us with a lattice top peach pie, and it was somethin' else.

A Moment of Respite

Sometime in November, things get a little crazy around here. Shopping for the holidays, shopping for Thanksgiving, cooking for Thanksgiving, coordinating family get-togethers, making sure everyone has a proper coat and hat and boots, shoveling snow, decorating the house, and on and on. Gets to be a bit much some days, and my answer to that is an evening with friends. Only this time, there's no dinner at the table. Instead, appetizers and desserts, all the way, and some fun to be had by all.

Baked Brie with Pepper Jelly

Spicy Bacon and Cheddar Chip Dip

Cranberry Meatballs

Baby Bella Brie Quiche

Cranberry Orange Scones

Raspberry Spice Fondue Dip

Sweet Almond Popcorn

Crème de Menthe Cake

Pecan Spritz

~ A FEW GOOD IDEAS FOR THE EVENING ~

DECOR . . . .

Place fresh pine boughs here and there, and lit apple-cinnamon candles. If it's not December yet, no need to rush: hold off on the holiday decorations.

TO KEEP THE CONVERSATION GOING . . . .

Almost everyone has an ugly Christmas or holiday sweater, and if you don't, they aren't hard to find. Invite your guests to wear theirs, and to bring an object for show-and-tell. Something with a story connected to it. After dinner, sit in the most cozy room for guests and do a show-and-tell. Old toys, jewelry, a box of chocolates, something of your grandfather's: everything has a story.

SOMETHING TO DO . . . .

Have an old fashioned sing-a-long. Pass out small instruments to add to the fun—finger cymbals, a triangle, jingle bells, a small drum, maracas, kazoos. Sing some traditional songs, or songs from childhood. Maybe a hymn, if you're feelin' it.

WHAT TO DRINK . . . .

Serve a hot drink we call a "Candy Cane." Mix together ⅓ oz Rumple Minze (a German peppermint liqueur) and ⅓ oz Baileys Irish Cream into 1 cup of hot chocolate. Cheers! For those who aren't up for alcohol, try this Holiday Punch: combine 2 cups of cranberry juice with 4 cups of ginger ale in a punch bowl. Stir, and throw a couple orange slices on top.

MAKE IT YOUR OWN . . . .

This is a good time of year for a cookie exchange, but make sure to make enough to give each guest a dozen. In our case, everyone went home with four dozen holiday cookies, more than enough to share with family and friends, or freeze. Also, an evening of relaxing doesn't rule out fun. Invite guests to bring boots and snow pants and to do a little night sledding at the best sledding hill nearby.

Baked Brie with Pepper Jelly

½ package puff pastry, thawed for about 40 minutes on the counter
1 (8 oz) wheel of baby Brie
About 3-4 T pepper jelly
1 egg white, mixed with about 2 tsp cold water

Preheat oven to 400. Gently unfold the puff pastry sheet. If it tears, gently mend it. Cut the Brie in half lengthwise and place one half, rind down, on the pastry. Spread with jelly and then place the other half of the Brie, rind up, on the jelly. If necessary, trim the excess pastry and then fold it over the cheese, sealing the edges. Turn over, so the seam is at the bottom. Decorate with decorative shapes cut from the excess dough and brush it with the egg white and water mixture. Place the bundle on a lightly greased baking dish. Bake for 15 to 20 minutes or until the pastry is golden brown. Serve with crackers, bread, and strawberries, apples, pears and grapes. A dish of dried cranberries is nice, too.

Spicy Bacon and Cheddar Chip Dip

8 slices bacon, chopped and crisped
8 oz softened cream cheese
½ cup bacon mayonnaise (regular mayo works, too)
2 tsp Dijon mustard
1½ cups shredded cheddar cheese
2 tsp chopped jalapeños
3 green onions, chopped
½ cup smoked almonds (optional)

Brown bacon in nonstick skillet over medium heat. Drain crisp bacon bits on paper towel. In a mixing bowl, combine cream cheese, mayo, Dijon mustard, cheddar, jalapeños and onion with cooked bacon.

Transfer to a shallow small casserole or baking dish and bake at 400 until golden brown and bubbly at edges, about 15 minutes. Top with chopped smoked almonds if desired. Serve with your favorite chips, crackers or vegetables. Try serving in a small, hollowed-out sourdough round.

Cranberry Meatballs

Meatballs

2 lbs lean ground beef
1 (1 or 2 oz) package dry onion soup mix
1 cup seasoned breadcrumbs
1 egg

Sauce

16 oz ketchup
16 oz water
1 cup brown sugar
1 (16 oz) can whole cranberry sauce
1 (16 oz) can sauerkraut, rinsed and drained

Combine all meatball ingredients and form into cocktail-sized balls. Place in a large, shallow roasting pan. For sauce, combine all ingredients in a saucepan and simmer 10 minutes. Pour over meatballs and bake at 350 for 1 hour. Keep warm in a covered ovenproof serving dish until serving. You may prepare these ahead of time and serve in a warm crock pot.

Baby Bella Brie Quiche

¾ cup chopped baby portobello mushrooms
¼ cup minced shallots
1 T butter
3 oz Brie cheese, rind removed and sliced
1 deep-dish pie shell
3 eggs, lightly beaten
1½ cups cream

Sauté the mushrooms and shallots in the butter. Set aside. Place the cheese in the bottom of the pie shell. Mix the eggs, cream and mushroom mixture together and pour into the shell. Place on a cookie sheet and bake at 375 for 25 to 30 minutes (or until the top is lightly browned and the pie is firm in the middle).

Serves 4 to 6.

Cranberry Orange Scones

1¾ cups all-purpose flour
1½ tsp baking powder
½ tsp baking soda
½ tsp salt
2 T sugar

1 stick cold unsalted butter
½ cup Craisins (dried cranberries)
Grated zest of an orange
Coarse sugar for sprinkling
⅔ cup buttermilk (plus extra for brushing)

Preheat oven to 400.

Mix flour, baking powder, baking soda, salt and sugar.

Cut the cold butter into small ¼- to ½-inch cubes. Mix with flour mixture until butter is just coated with flour, leaving large chunks. Stir in the cranberries and the zest. (You may want to briefly soak dried fruits in hot water or rum, then drain and toss in sugar before adding).

Stir in ⅔ cup buttermilk and mix just until the liquid is absorbed and the batter begins to pull away from the sides of the bowl. Scrape the dough down with a spatula and form into a ball.

Flatten the dough into a circle ¾ inch thick, and place on a baking sheet lined with parchment paper, a silicone baking sheet or a buttered sheet of wax paper. Divide the circle into eight wedges and separate the wedges out, leaving a ½-inch space between them.

Brush the tops with remaining buttermilk (or egg white). Sprinkle with coarse sugar. Bake 15–20 minutes or until lightly browned. Dust scones with confectioner's sugar, if desired, and serve warm with butter and jam or honey.

Raspberry Spice Fondue Dip

2 (10 oz) packages frozen sweetened raspberries
2 cups apple butter
2 T cinnamon red hots
4 tsp cornstarch
Pinch of cinnamon
Fresh fruit

Thaw and drain raspberries, reserving 2 T juice. Mash raspberries, and press through a fine-mesh strainer into a small saucepan; discard seeds.

Add apple butter and red hots to raspberries; cook over medium heat until candies are dissolved, stirring now and then. Combine cornstarch and reserved juice until smooth; stir into berry mixture with a pinch of cinnamon. Bring to a boil; cook and stir over medium heat for a minute or two, or until thickened.

Serve warm in a small fondue pot or refrigerate until chilled and serve cold. Serve with fruit.

Makes about 2 cups.

Sweet Almond Popcorn

2 bags of microwave popcorn, popped
1 (5 oz) bag dried cranberries
1 (2 oz) bag sliced almonds
2 cups white chocolate chips, melted

Combine popcorn, dried cranberries and almonds. Pour melted chocolate over and stir well. Spread over a cookie sheet lined with wax paper. Cool.

Break into bite-sized pieces. Store in an airtight container.

Crème de Menthe Cake

1 white cake mix
¼ cup plus 2 tsp crème de menthe
1 (16 oz) jar Hershey fudge sauce
8 oz Cool Whip

Mix cake according to directions, but substitute ¼ cup crème de menthe for ¼ cup of the water. Bake according to directions, and cool.

Gently spread fudge sauce over. For frosting, mix 2 tsp crème de menthe with Cool Whip and spread over cake.

Note: This recipe can be made a day ahead of time.

Pecan Spritz

    1 cup sugar
    1½ cups butter
    1 egg
    1 tsp vanilla
    ½ tsp almond extract
    3 cups flour
    1 cup ground pecans
    1 tsp baking powder
    12 oz white chocolate chips, optional

Cream sugar and butter together; mix in egg, vanilla, almond extract. Add flour, ground pecans and baking powder. Stir well. Chill awhile. Add a bit of flour to hands while hand-mixing dough. Fill cookie press, and shoot cookies out onto an ungreased baking sheet.

Bake at 375 for 5 to 7 minutes.

When cool, dip half of cookie in melted white chips, if desired.

Enjoy!

HOW IT ALL WENT

Invited some friends over Saturday, and it was a good time. It was kind of a spontaneous thing, so I suggested everyone bring an appetizer or a dessert, along with some sledding clothes and an object with a story. To my surprise, everyone wanted to go sledding right away instead of after dinner. We headed over to the Lutheran church, which has a hill behind it, but nothing too extreme, and we brought the kids' sleds and each took several runs down the hill. My gosh, that was fun. In an attempt to avoid plowing over Mrs. Hansen, Mr. Sundberg swerved and nearly smashed into a telephone pole. First time I ever heard the man scream. After everyone had their fill, we headed in to a really fine spread.

My favorite part of the evening was listening to the stories behind the objects people brought. Mrs. Hansen had a photo of her father, and she talked about how he was a banker and fought in WW II. Mr. Lund brought the first shirt Mrs. Lund ever gave him and told about how he had proposed. He was wearing that shirt, and she interrupted him with a big ol' yes. Mr. Ableidinger brought some cheese and told us how it's the stinkiest cheese there is, then offered it to us. (That's when I got the mint cake out.) Mr. Sundberg showed us the collection of his woodcarvings, and Mr. Stendahl brought a first edition copy of Robert Frost's poems. I could have listened all night to those stories of ordinary, beautiful lives.

A Holiday Progressive Dinner

Days grow dark earlier now, and there are lights shimmering all 'round town, and the scent of pine is in the air. It's time to get out and celebrate, to gather together despite the sub-zero temperatures, to have friends over now that the tree is up and the star is lit, and to raise a glass in a toast to good friends and health and peace on earth. A progressive dinner is just the thing. Each course is prepared and served at the home of a different host, a traveling potluck of good tidings and cheer.

Hot Spiced Cranberry Cider

Spinach Artichoke Dip

Bacon-Wrapped Shrimp

Holiday Waldorf Salad

Beef Stroganoff

Wild Rice Casserole

Rum Cake

Ruth's Cranberry Christmas Cake

Cream Cheese Delights

~ A FEW GOOD IDEAS FOR THE EVENING ~

DECOR . . . .

Given that it's the holiday season, you'll see the homes of your friends done up all festive. Play a different holiday CD at each of the four houses you visit, something that fits the mood of the meal's course. Try to fit in Handel's "Messiah" somewhere along the way.

TO KEEP THE CONVERSATION GOING . . . .

Each host might provide a gift of an ornament for each person/couple attending. When the evening is over, you'll take home four different ornaments for the tree. During dinner, tell tales from Christmases past. Share favorite Christmas moments, and stories of holidays when you were a child.

SOMETHING TO DO . . . .

Bring a wrapped gift that starts with the first letter of your name. Keep 'em in the car until you get to the last house. Pile 'em up in the corner, and find a creative way to decide who chooses when. Alphabetical order, rolling dice, etc. After each gift is opened, the opener has to say who he or she thinks the giver is.

WHAT TO DRINK . . . .

Each host should offer a different beverage. Coffee ought to show up somewhere, and a host's favorite wine is always nice. Homemade mint cordial is a lovely drink for dessert. To make it, pour the following into a blender: 1 (14 oz) can sweetened condensed milk, 1½ cups whipping cream, 1 cup of peppermint schnapps and 2 tsp vanilla. Blend 'til smooth, and chill, shaking it up before serving.

MAKE IT YOUR OWN . . . .

Consider establishing a dinner tradition. We pass a fruitcake along. The fruitcake was old to start, and we find clever ways to pass it on from one household to another. The only rule? You have to keep it for a year. Oh, and no sampling the fruitcake.

Hot Spiced Cranberry Cider

2 quarts apple cider
6 cups cranberry juice
¼ cup packed brown sugar
4 cinnamon sticks
1½ tsp whole cloves
1 lemon, thinly sliced

Combine all ingredients in a large pot. Bring to a boil, reduce heat and simmer for 15 to 20 minutes. With a slotted spoon, remove cinnamon, cloves and lemon slices. Serve hot.

Makes 25 servings.

Spinach Artichoke Dip

1 (10 oz) package spinach
1 (13 oz) can artichoke hearts
12 oz cream cheese, softened
1 cup Parmesan cheese
½ cup mayonnaise
3 large garlic cloves, pressed
2 T lemon juice

Drain spinach. Press between layers of paper towel to remove excess moisture.

Combine all ingredients in a bowl. Stir well. Spoon into a lightly greased 11x7 baking dish, or a casserole, or what have you.

Bake at 375 for about 25 minutes. Serve with assorted crackers, bagel chips or breadsticks.

Makes 4 cups dip.

Optional: Mix 2 T melted butter with 1½ cups breadcrumbs. (You can make breadcrumbs by pulsing chunks of a French baguette in a food processor.) Sprinkle over dip before baking.

Bacon-Wrapped Shrimp

1 pound large shrimp
⅓ cup chopped fresh basil
1½ T freshly grated Parmesan cheese
2-3 garlic cloves, minced
16 pieces thinly sliced bacon
½ cup prepared barbecue sauce (fruit-based is best)

Peel and devein shrimp, leaving tails on. Butterfly shrimp by cutting a slit along the back and gently pressing open.

Combine basil, Parmesan and garlic in a small bowl. Gently pack basil mixture evenly in shrimp openings; press shrimp closed.

Cook bacon over medium heat until partially cooked. Drain on paper towels. Wrap each shrimp with 1 slice bacon and place on greased baking sheet. Brush barbecue sauce over shrimp, and bake at 400 for 8 to 9 minutes.

Holiday Waldorf Salad

2 medium red apples, chopped
2 medium green apples, chopped
2 T lemon juice
½ cup sliced celery
½ cup chopped walnuts
½ cup raisins (or dried cranberries)
1 cup mayo (or ½ cup mayo and ½ cup whipping cream)
1-2 tsp sugar
Dash of salt
A bit of cinnamon
A bit of nutmeg

In medium bowl, toss apples with lemon juice. Add celery and nuts; stir and set aside. Combine mayo, sugar and salt. Fold into apple mixture. Sprinkle with a bit of cinnamon and nutmeg.

Makes 6 servings.

Beef Stroganoff

2 lbs beef tenderloin or sirloin
4 T flour
1 (16 oz) carton sour cream
4 T instant beef bouillon granules
1 cup water
½ tsp pepper
4 T butter

2-3 cups sliced mushrooms
  (baby bellas are my favorite)
1 cup chopped yellow onion
2-3 cloves garlic, minced
2-3 T cooking sherry, or to taste
4 cups hot cooked noodles

Slice beef across the grain into thin, bite-size strips. (Works best if meat is partially frozen.) Combine the flour and sour cream. Dissolve bouillon granules in water, and add pepper, and stir into sour cream mixture. Set aside.

In a large skillet, cook and stir half the meat in the butter over high heat until meat is done.

Remove the meat and set aside. Add remaining meat, mushrooms, onion and garlic to skillet. Cook, stirring occasionally, 'til the meat is done and the onion is tender. Add the meat you've already cooked and pour the sour cream mixture over. Add cooking sherry. Cook and stir over medium heat until bubbly, and then a minute or two more.

Serve over hot cooked noodles.

Serves 8.

Wild Rice Casserole

½ stick butter
½ onion, chopped
4 oz fresh mushrooms, sliced
1 cup wild rice
3 cups hot chicken broth
¼ cup chopped cashews, optional

Heat butter in a frying pan over low heat. Sauté onions and mushrooms. Add the wild rice and blend all together. Transfer to a greased casserole dish and add chicken broth.

Cover and bake at 350 degrees for 45 minutes or until all liquid is absorbed.

Garnish with chopped cashews.

Rum Cake

½ cup chopped nuts
 (pecans or almonds are good)
1 yellow pudding cake mix
4 eggs
½ cup oil
½ cup cold water
½ cup rum

Sauce

½ cup melted butter
1 cup sugar
¼ cup rum
¼ cup water

Grease a bundt pan, and sprinkle nuts on the bottom.

Beat together cake mix, eggs, oil, water and rum. Pour over nuts. Bake at 325 for 55 to 60 minutes.

Combine sauce ingredients and pour over baked cake while it's still in the pan. Let sit half an hour or so, and invert onto plate.

Serve with freshly whipped cream.

Ruth's Cranberry Christmas Cake

1 cup sugar
3 T butter
½ cup water
½ cup evaporated milk
2 cups flour
2 tsp baking soda
1 tsp salt
2 cups cranberries

Cream together sugar and 3 T butter and set aside. Mix together water and ½ cup evaporated milk. Combine with sugar and butter mixture. Add flour, baking soda and salt. Beat well. Fold in cranberries. Bake for 30 to 35 minutes at 350.

Serve warm, with butter sauce.

Butter Sauce

2 sticks butter
2 cups sugar
1 cup evaporated milk
2 tsp vanilla

Melt butter in medium saucepan, and add sugar. Stir well. Add evaporated milk and vanilla. Cook over low heat, stirring until sugar dissolves. Serve hot over warm cake.

Cream Cheese Delights

1⅓ cups flour
¼ tsp baking powder
½ tsp salt
1 (8 oz) package cream cheese, softened
1 stick unsalted butter, softened
1 cup sugar
1 tsp vanilla extract
1 large egg
¾ cup rainbow sprinkles (or colored sugar)

In a medium bowl sift together flour, baking powder and salt. In a separate bowl, beat cream cheese and butter until smooth. Add sugar gradually and mix until light and fluffy. Add vanilla and egg and beat well. Add the dry ingredients to the cream cheese mixture and stir until just combined. Do not overmix. Chill batter 2 hours or overnight.

Preheat oven to 350. Line two baking sheets with parchment paper. Add ½ the sprinkles to a wide shallow bowl (add more as needed). Scoop up rounded tablespoons of dough and form into balls. They may not be perfect, as the dough is sticky; try wetting your hands lightly. Drop into the sprinkles and coat all sides, and place on baking sheet 2 inches apart.

Bake 12–14 minutes until lightly golden on the bottom. Cool on baking sheets 10 minutes or so.

Enjoy!

HOW IT ALL WENT

Invited some friends over Saturday, and it was a good time. It was a progressive dinner, and Mr. Sundberg and I were the first stop for appetizers. Everyone came a bit more dressed up than usual, wearing fancy blouses and wool sweaters and ties. It's nice to feel elegant now and then, and when you have only one course to prepare, it's easier to dress up. I made some spiced cider, artichoke dip, and some bacon-wrapped shrimp.

Mr. Ableidinger, bless his heart, rented a van so we could all travel together. He had picked up everyone on the way to our place and drove us over to the Stendahls'. This was his contribution, as a pipe burst in his kitchen, and he couldn't host. We arrived at the Stendahls' and had some wonderful Waldorf salad with cranberries and walnuts, Mrs. Stendahl's own recipe. Then on to the Hansens', for beef stroganoff and wild rice casserole.

Our final stop was the Lunds', for dessert. That was something. Mrs. Lund had arranged a table plumb full of delicious. There was cranberry cake with butter sauce, rum cake with whipped topping, a large platter of cookies, and a tiered platter of candies and fudge. We filled our plates one last time, sat in the living room and played our choose-a-gift game. Things grew quiet, and Mrs. Stendahl hummed at first, and then began to sing, "Silent Night." Mr. Sundberg took my hand in his, and we sat there awhile, each among friends, and I felt it. The Christmas Spirit, to be sure.

Back in the Day

Remember when you were in high school and you walked home after practice and there was homemade macaroni and cheese waiting on the stove? Remember when you and your friends hung out at the malt shop and shared malts and plates of fries and listened to the jukebox laughing together 'til your mom honked the horn outside? And how you came home Saturday after a day out cutting wood with your dad, and your mom had a batch of caramel corn in the oven, and there on the counter was that cheese ball? You know the one. Food can take us back, and as we turn the corner into a New Year, why not go there? You know, way back when.

Savory Sausage Bites

Cream Cheese Pickle Roll-ups

Festive Cheese Ball

Ham 'n' Swiss Sandwiches

Baked Sweet Potato Fries

Grandma's Peanut Bars

Caramel Corn

Light and Puffy Chocolate Chip Cookies

Beer Batter Waffles

~ A FEW GOOD IDEAS FOR THE EVENING ~

DECOR . . . .

Use lots of balloons or streamers. Go with one color, school colors, or multicolor. Everyone should dress like they did in high school. Hairstyles included.

TO KEEP THE CONVERSATION GOING . . . . . .

Request that your guests bring CDs or albums (make sure you've got a record player set up) of the best and worst music from back in the day. Play some of it while you're eating, and have everyone share memories of their worst/best moments back in high school.

SOMETHING TO DO . . . .

Play a game called "Who Do You Think?" This one takes a bit of prep work. From each person at the party collect a statement that was true about them when they were back in high school. (Example: I played the lead in "My Fair Lady.") The statement should be something no one in the group knows. Type up the statements along with the names of the guests and have people match 'em up. Read the statements aloud, and have each person stand up when his or her statement is read. Whoever gets the most right wins the bottle of champagne!

WHAT TO DRINK . . . .

Take it back in time. Offer up chocolate malts, cherry Cokes and cream soda. Some homemade root beer would be good if someone wants to give it a whirl.

MAKE IT YOUR OWN . . . .

Invite guests to bring food that takes them back. Anything goes, no questions asked.

And dance. Make it a '50s dance, or figure out the year each person in the group graduated from high school, and gather up music from that decade. Play it loud, and maybe have a little dance contest.

Savory Sausage Bites

1 lb Jimmy Dean hot sausage
1 lb ground beef
1 lb Velveeta, cut up in small chunks
Salt, pepper and parsley, to taste
Cocktail rye bread

Brown sausage and ground beef in skillet; mix well and drain. Add Velveeta and melt it with the meat, mixing well. Add salt, pepper and parsley, to taste. Spread on cocktail rye bread and place on a cookie sheet.

Bake at 350 for 12 to 15 minutes, and serve.

Note: These snacks freeze well when stored in a Ziploc bag.

Cream Cheese Pickle Roll-ups

1 (8 oz) package cream cheese, softened
1½ lb sliced honey-roasted ham
1 jar dill pickles (not little ones)

Spread thin layer of cream cheese on a slice of meat. Cut pickles lengthwise into quarters. (Pre-cut spears will work, too.) Wrap pickle quarter with the cheese-covered meat slice. Keep spreading the cheese on ham slices and wrapping the pickle spears up in them.

Place in a plastic container or on a serving platter and chill for at least 1 hour, then slice rolls into wheels and stick toothpicks in them for serving. You'll have a pickle slice wrapped in cream cheese and ham. Yum!

Festive Cheese Ball

½ lb grated white cheddar
3 oz cream cheese
3 T sherry
¼ cup pitted ripe or green olives
½ tsp Worcestershire sauce
Dashes of onion, garlic and celery salts
½ cup chopped dried beef

Combine all ingredients except beef. Form ball. Wrap in plastic and refrigerate. About half an hour before serving, unwrap and roll in dried beef until covered well.

Ham 'n' Swiss Sandwiches

2 (12 count) packages sweet Hawaiian dinner rolls
1½ lbs Virginia ham, thinly sliced
12 slices Swiss cheese
1 stick butter
2-3 tsp Worcestershire sauce
1 tsp garlic powder or minced garlic
1 tsp onion powder or minced onion
1 tsp poppy seeds or sesame seeds

Place the bottoms of 12 rolls in each of two 9x13 cake pans.

Place ham (about 2 shaved slices or so) onto each of the rolls. Cut cheese slices into 4 parts and place 2 small pieces on each sandwich, and place the dinner roll tops on.

In a saucepan, mix butter, Worcestershire sauce, onion powder, garlic powder and poppy seeds. Wait until all butter is melted and then brush the melted mixture over the ham sandwiches. Cover with foil and let sit in fridge for an hour or overnight.

Bake uncovered at 375 for 15 minutes or until cheese is melted. Serve hot or cold.

Baked Sweet Potato Fries

4 medium-sized sweet potatoes
1-2 T olive oil
½ tsp salt
Pepper

Wash potatoes and pat dry with a paper towel. Cut each lengthwise into four, and each fourth into two or three, depending on how thick you want your fries. Toss with a tablespoon or two of olive oil, and a half teaspoon or so of salt. Spread over foil-lined or spray-coated baking sheet and bake at 425 for 15 minutes. Turn fries over with fork and bake another 10–15 minutes. Pepper, to taste.

Grandma's Peanut Bars

3 eggs
1 cup sugar
4 T water, cold
1½ cups flour
1 tsp baking powder
2 cups or so ground peanuts

Frosting

1 T butter
⅓ cup milk
1 tsp vanilla
5 cups or so powdered sugar

Beat eggs and sugar 5–10 minutes or so, depending on how aggressive you're feelin'. Add water and mix, then flour and baking powder. Bake 20 minutes at 350. Cut into bars. Frost with powdered sugar frosting. Roll in ground peanuts.

For powdered sugar frosting, melt butter with milk in microwave. Add vanilla. Pour about 5 cups of powdered sugar in a bowl, add butter mixture gradually, stirring as you go, until frosting is thick but not too thick. You can always thin it out with milk or add more powdered sugar. Spread over cake pieces with a butter knife 'til they're coated, and roll in ground peanuts.

Caramel Corn

6 quarts popped popcorn
2 sticks butter
2 cups brown sugar
½ cup white corn syrup
1 tsp salt
1 tsp baking soda
1 tsp butter flavoring

Pop the popcorn, and set aside in a large bowl.

Melt butter in a medium saucepan, over medium heat. Add brown sugar, syrup and salt. Bring to a boil, stirring constantly, and then boil for 4 minutes without stirring. Remove from heat. Add baking soda and butter flavor. Stir well. Pour over popped corn and mix well. Spread over foil on a baking sheet. Bake at 200 for 1 hour, stirring every 15 minutes.

Store covered.

Light and Puffy Chocolate Chip Cookies

1 cup brown sugar
1 cup white sugar
1 cup shortening
1 cup oil
2 eggs
1 tsp vanilla
4¼ cups flour
2 tsp soda
4 tsp cream of tartar
1 tsp salt
2 cups chocolate chips

Cream together the first four ingredients. Stir in eggs and vanilla. Add flour, soda, cream of tartar and salt and mix well; add chips.

Bake at 350 on foil-lined cookie sheets, 8–10 minutes or until the cookies look the way you want 'em to.

Beer Batter Waffles

2¼ cups flour
3 T sugar
½ tsp salt
6 T butter, melted
2 eggs, lightly beaten
1 tsp vanilla
2 tsp orange rind, freshly grated
1 T orange juice
1 (12 oz) can beer, your favorite

In large bowl, combine flour, sugar and salt. Melt butter and let cool.

Add all remaining ingredients, butter included, to flour mixture all at once. Beat 'til smooth. Let batter rest a good hour at room temperature. Stir gently before using. Top with fresh fruit, whipped cream, or some lingonberry sauce.

Enjoy!

HOW IT ALL WENT

Invited some friends over Saturday, and it was a good time. It was New Year's Eve, and I've been wanting to have a dance party, and at long last Mr. Sundberg agreed. I was a bit worn out from all the holiday cooking, and figured I'd switch it up and make it a high school potluck of sorts. I went with simple ham sandwiches and sweet potato fries, a little variation on my favorite meal back when I was a senior.

Everyone was in. They showed up dressed like they did back in the day. We didn't all attend high school at the same time, which made things interesting. There were outfits from the late 60s, 70s and early 80s. Mrs. Lund had big, puffed out hair, and Mrs. Stendahl wore hers in braids, and Mr. Ableidinger wore his hair all slicked back. Mr. Sundberg skipped his haircut last week so he looked a bit shaggy, and I, well, I guess my hair hasn't changed all that much. I clipped a barrette just over my temple and that did the trick. We all looked a little bit like aliens and that was okay by me.

The array of food was interesting, all delicious, though I thought Mr. Stendahl's contribution of beer batter waffles with lingonberries and whipped cream for dessert was a bit odd. He explained that it's what his dad made every Saturday night for dinner, and, well, who can argue? And, truth be told, after all the games and dancing and whooping it up, at midnight, those beer batter waffles tasted mighty dang fine.

Chinese New Year

It's been a long, cold winter, and it's not over yet, and we all need a reason to go out. Thank goodness for the Chinese New Year. The celebration starts with the new moon on the first day of the New Year and ends fifteen days later, on the full moon. That's over two weeks of festivities, but all you really need is one evening together with friends and an amazing array of good, homemade Chinese food.

Crab Rangoon

Egg Rolls with Dipping Sauce

Hoisin Pork Wraps

Cashew Chicken with Noodles

Chicken Fried Rice

Almond Cookies

~ A FEW GOOD IDEAS FOR THE EVENING ~

DECOR . . . .

Simplicity is the key. As the color red is considered good luck in China, lay down a red tablecloth or table runner, and hang a red banner over the door. Do a little research, draw the Chinese characters for happiness on cardstock with the names of your guests, and place one on each plate. Set out a bowl of oranges and tangerines, which represent abundant happiness. Hang a few colorful Chinese lanterns, and make sure you have tea cups and chopsticks to go 'round.

TO KEEP THE CONVERSATION GOING . . . .

Print out the characters and meanings of the Chinese zodiac. Have everyone share what animal they are, and what qualities are associated with that animal, and point out the current year's symbol.

SOMETHING TO DO . . . .

Have a little contest with chopsticks. Place about ten items on a tray that need to be transferred to an empty tray using chopsticks. Trays should be a good 7–8 inches apart. Include items like cotton balls, macaroni noodles, a small carrot, eggs, etc. Whoever gets the most without dropping one, wins.

WHAT TO DRINK . . . .

Serve several varieties of tea, some green, black, oolong or white. Visit a liquor store where you'll find a selection of rice wine, and pick up a few different varieties so guests can sample each.

MAKE IT YOUR OWN . . . .

Chinese desserts are simple, like custard or ice cream, and often there is no dessert. Make some almond cookies yourself, or make a visit to a Chinese grocery or the international aisle at your grocery store, and pick up a variety of Chinese sweets and perhaps a cake to set out after the meal, along with some fortune cookies.

Crab Rangoon

4 oz Neufchâtel cheese
¼ cup mayo (light works)
1 can crab meat
2 green onions, chopped
1 package wonton wraps (or use egg roll wraps cut into four squares)

Combine first four ingredients. Add a heavy teaspoon of filling to each wonton wrap. Moisten edges of wrap and fold up corners together. Give a little twist, or make it more like an envelope, whatever works for you. Place one crab Rangoon in each cup of a lightly oiled muffin tin.

Bake in 350 oven 20 minutes or so.

Egg Rolls with Dipping Sauce

½ lb ground pork

1 small carrot, shaved

1 small onion, finely chopped

4 oz finely chopped mushrooms, optional

¼ tsp pepper

A dash MSG

A dash or two garlic powder

4 T soy sauce

¼ tsp Tabasco

2 cups shredded cabbage

1 egg, beaten

1 small bundle bean threads (big handful), soaked in hot water 'til soft, drained and chopped

Paste of cornstarch and water in small bowl

1 package egg roll wraps

3 cups oil, heated hot in wok or deep frying pan

Dipping Sauce

3 T soy sauce

1½ tsp sesame oil

3 T vinegar

1½ tsp sugar

Cook pork in saucepan; drain off fat. In large bowl, combine pork, carrot, onion, mushrooms, pepper, MSG, garlic powder, soy, Tabasco and cabbage. Mix well. Add egg and bean threads. Mix again. Spoon 1 large T filling (drain off excess juice) onto center of an egg roll wrap set in a diamond shape in front of you. Fold lower corner up over filling and tuck under filling. Fold left side onto rolled wrap, and then right side, using cornstarch paste to glue it. Roll while pulling top flap over, tucking and sealing again. (Think of it as making an envelope.) Place egg roll seam-side down into hot oil. Fry 'til brown on each side. Remove, and place on platter covered with several layers of paper towel. Keep warm in oven until done frying. Serve with dipping sauce. To make dipping sauce, stir sauce ingredients together in small bowl.

Hoisin Pork Wraps

2 small cucumbers, thinly sliced
½ tsp sugar
¼ tsp salt
1½ lb thin boneless pork loin chops
1 T toasted sesame oil
Salt
Pepper
3 green onions
8 tortillas
1 small jar hoisin sauce

Toss cucumbers, sugar and salt in medium bowl; set aside.

Heat skillet to medium high. Rub pork chops with toasted sesame oil; sprinkle with salt and pepper. Cook pork 3 to 4 minutes each side or until cooked through. Slice onions thinly at an angle, and set aside. Wrap tortillas in damp paper towels and microwave a minute or two until warm and soft.

Drain cucumbers and thinly slice the pork. Place pork in tortillas; top with cucumbers and green onions. Drizzle each with a teaspoon or two of hoisin sauce. Serve with hoisin sauce on the side.

Cashew Chicken with Noodles

16 oz uncooked thick rice noodles
½ cup soy sauce
4 T cornstarch
6 garlic cloves, minced
2 lbs boneless, skinless chicken breasts, cubed

2-3 T peanut oil
2-3 T sesame oil
9 green onions, cut into 2-inch pieces
2 cups unsalted cashews
4 T sweet chili sauce

Cook rice noodles according to package directions. Meanwhile, in a small bowl, combine the soy sauce, cornstarch and garlic. Add chicken. In a large skillet, sauté chicken mixture in peanut and sesame oils until no longer pink. Add onions; cook 1 minute longer. Drain noodles; stir into skillet. Add cashews and chili sauce and heat through. Serves about 8.

Chicken Fried Rice

8 T vegetable oil, divided
2 eggs
½ cup diced chicken
½ cup peas, optional
4 cups cooked rice (rinse before cooking)

¼ cup chopped green onion
2 tsp salt
½ tsp sugar
3 T soy sauce

Heat 2 T oil in wok. Pour in beaten eggs and stir fry into tiny pieces. Remove. Heat 3 T oil in wok. Stir fry meat a few minutes until cooked. Add peas and stir fry a minute more. Remove. Heat 3 T oil. Stir fry onion and cooked rice. Sprinkle in salt, sugar and soy, and continue stirring. Reduce heat and stir 'til rice is heated. Add eggs and chicken (and peas, if applicable), and stir thoroughly.

Almond Cookies

2¾ cups flour
1 cup white sugar
½ tsp baking soda
½ tsp salt
1 cup lard (butter works, too)
1 egg
1½ tsp almond extract
48 almonds

Preheat oven to 325.

Combine flour, sugar, baking soda and salt together into a bowl. Cut in the lard until mixture resembles cornmeal. Add egg and almond extract. Mix well.

Roll dough into 1-inch balls. Set them 2 inches apart on an ungreased cookie sheet. Place an almond on top of each cookie and press down a bit to flatten.

Bake at 325 'til the edges of the cookies are golden brown, 15 to 17 minutes.

HOW IT ALL WENT

Invited some friends over Saturday, and it was a good time. It was one of those evenings where we didn't do much at all except sit and eat and talk, and there were no complaints. It takes the better part of January for things to normalize, and then the polar wind-chills return and there isn't much to do but stay in and bake and plan things and read.

We got to reminiscing about all the years we've been getting together, and a few of the more memorable gatherings. There was the time Mr. Ableidinger broke his leg, and we brought take-out Korean to his hospital room and sat there eating kimchi while he, sedated, talked nonsense and made us all laugh. And the time the Hansens renewed their vows in the park and we grilled chicken and attempted a maypole dance. And then there was the evening out on the trampoline.

We sat down to eat, and just as we began, Mr. Sundberg cleared his throat. "I'd like to say something, if you all don't mind." For a motivational speaker, he's a bit uneasy when it comes speaking in small groups. "Well, we're celebrating the end of another year of knowing each other, and looking toward a new year ahead." He raised his glass of rice wine. "Here's to friendship, and to you, my friends. I'm blessed to know you. May we always make time to gather together." We clinked our glasses and drank, and the feasting began.

About the Author

At age 9, in the back seat of her grandmother's car on the way to a funeral, Holly Harden began to write, and she's been writing ever since. She grew up in Wisconsin, where she baked and cooked with her mother, father and grandmothers, and where her parents hosted frequent gatherings of friends. She majored in English at St. Olaf College, and taught secondary English for nine years before she earned, in 2002, an MFA in Writing from Hamline University. Holly's nonfiction has appeared in *Utne* and *Fourth Genre*, and she edited Garrison Keillor's *Life Among the Lutherans*. This is her second cookbook; her first, *Good Food from Mrs. Sundberg's Kitchen*, was published by Adventure Publications in the spring of 2014. Holly lives in Minnesota, where she writes for *A Prairie Home Companion*, teaches writing classes, and helps her three children get where they're going.

Photo by Tom Roster

Notes